OF, BY, AND FOR LIBRARIANS

Second Series

CONTRIBUTIONS TO LIBRARY LITERATURE

John David Marshall, *General Editor*

Of, By, and for Librarians

SECOND SERIES

Selected by

JOHN DAVID MARSHALL

THE SHOE STRING PRESS, INC.

HAMDEN, CONNECTICUT

1974

Library of Congress Cataloging in Publication Data

Marshall, John David, 1928-   comp.
    Of, by and for librarians: second series.

    (Contributions to library literature, no. 10)
    1. Library science — Addresses, essays, lectures. I. Title.
    Z665.M663   020'.8   73-16428
    ISBN 0-208-01333-4

Copyright © 1974 by The Shoe String Press, Inc.
995 Sherman Avenue, Hamden, Connecticut 06514

Printed in the United States of America

For the STEWARTS

> *Mary*
> *Marshall*
> *Gladys*
> *Jim*

CONTENTS

BY WAY OF INTRODUCTION

A number of adjectives — not all of them complimentary — have been used to describe library literature. That much of the literature of librarianship is dull, repetitious, poorly written, or worse can hardly be denied. There is, however, a substantial body of library literature which should not be so characterized. There are both within and without the profession authors who have contributed lively, well-written, thought-provoking essays and articles dealing with books and libraries, librarians and librarianship.

In *Books-Libraries-Librarians* (1955) and *Of, By, and For Librarians* (1960), I attempted to bring together a selection of some of the better contributions which have been made to library literature. These two anthologies were generally well received and favorably reviewed. Since the publication of these two collections, I have continued to collect as something of a professional hobby articles and essays which — because of their point of view, style, content, treatment — particularly appealed to me. From this accumulation I have drawn the pieces that make up *Of, By, and For Librarians: Second Series.* I would like to hope that readers of this volume will find the selections included both appealing and enjoyable reading.

Of, By, and For Librarians: Second Series brings together from a variety of sources a selection of articles and essays that, hopefully, will make the reader aware of the unified diveristy of books and libraries and also aware of the combined fascination and responsibility which librarianship as a profession encompasses. Some twenty authors are represented in this collection. Most of the pieces included are by librarians. Some are by writers who — while not librarians — have written essays and articles that appropriately belong in part at least to the literature of librarianship. These authors have written well of and for librarians.

The anthologist always invites upon himself a slightly unfair kind of criticism: criticism for what he omitted as well as for what he included. Such criticism is one of the hazards which he must accept as inevitable when he embarks upon an adventure in anthology. If he attempts to explain why certain items were chosen and others not, he becomes defensive and perhaps even apologetic.

The first requirement for an anthologist, it seems to me, should be an enthusiasm for his subject and for the pieces dealing with his subject which he has selected for inclusion in his anthology. He should include only those items that he really likes and has enjoyed reading and re-reading — which means, of course, that he does each anthology for himself as well as for others. He naturally hopes that these others will like most, if not all, of what he likes. *Of, By, and For Librarians: Second Series,* then, reflects this anthologist's tastes, interests, healthy prejudices in his professional reading. It includes pieces that he believes merit preservation between the covers of a book.

Most anthologists, I suspect, encounter certain frustrations in pursuing the art and craft of anthologizing. This anthologist, fortunately, has a considerate and understanding publisher.

I gratefully note here and specifically acknowledge elsewhere the right to reprint the articles and essays included in this volume. To the authors, the original publishers, and/or their representatives go my thanks for granting permission to reprint.

My sincere thanks must also go to numerous friends and colleagues who, through the years, have encouraged me in my various anthologizing activities. They know who they are without my naming them.

—JOHN DAVID MARSHALL

September 7, 1973

BOOKS

AND

LIBRARIES

WILL THE BOOK SURVIVE?

Barbara Home Stewart

When the radio was invented, book publishers feared for the future. When the talking movie was perfected, book publishers were seriously disturbed. And when television sets began to dominate the scene, book publishers thought the end was in sight. But when tape cassettes appeared, they knew they were doomed.

Yet the humble book lives on and on and on.

It is easily installed without any service charge. It requires no extension cords or batteries. It pulls no amps so it can never blow a fuse, except emotionally. There is no service contract to be signed, no extra charges for house visits to repair it. Given reasonable care, no parts need ever be replaced. An eraser and a bit of scotch tape will do the job nicely, nine times out of ten. It requires no adjustment of the bass, treble, tone, balance, horizontal or vertical hold, color, or volume. Its head never needs to be cleaned.

A book can be operated under a wide spectrum of light conditions, as wide as that of the human eye. It is compact, lightweight and totally portable. It can be shipped anywhere in the world at the lowest postal rates. It can be stored or shipped in almost any size container. It can be used anywhere in the world, at any time, under almost any conditions— primitive or civilized—with or without electricity, in total seclusion or surrounded by crowds of people. When it is out-dated, it often becomes more valuable.

A book is an instrument of learning or a device of pleasure. It brings knowledge and joy to thousands of people, regardless of their age, sex, race, health, religion, income, or social position. It is accepted and appreciated as a symbol of prestige, friendship, affection or love in every country and in every language of the world. Its return to its original owner—after however many years—can often cement a broken friendship.

Books are almost as old as mankind. They have been found carved on the rocks of ageless mountains, painted on scrolls buried in caves, burned into animal hides in ancient desert tombs or carved into clay plaques in crumbling jungle temples. They will be found by men of the future when they tear apart the cornerstones of the buildings we live in today.

A book's uses are many and its costs are small. But there is one danger, and one danger only: it is highly addictive. Once you have mastered its use, you are hooked forever. Whether you live on a mountaintop, in a city or in a prison cell, you will find no cure for reading a book.

So beware of this small package, this book. It will change your life forever, and *it will endure.*   □

ON READING BOOKS

G. D. Lillibridge

I am very fond of books. Books to me are very much like
women. The come in all sizes and shapes—small, large, slim,
fat. Their moods are infinitely varied—playful, serious, coy,
dangerous. Their covers are designed to entice you to see
what lies within. They make delightful bedtime companions.
The scope of their capacity to influence men is astounding—
they can change a man's drinking habits or the very course of
history. Their content encompasses the range of the human
potential. Some you can get through in a few minutes, others
you spend a lifetime with and still you have not discovered
all they have to offer. In short, books are very much like
women, for in their presence the senses often reel, and in one
way or another they all have something to offer.

The great advantage, however, of books over women is
that it is possible to be a polygamist with books and not meet
the disfavor of the law or the reproach of society. It is true
that occasionally my college library in a tone highly sugges-
tive of disapproval wishes to know why it is that I keep
certain books in my harem years beyond the date I checked
them out. I take the view, however, that possession is nine-
tenths of the law— a rule of thumb, by the way, you can't
apply to women.

I make these remarks to establish my reputation as a

Reprinted from *California Librarian*, 29: 51-56, January 1968, by permission of the author and the publisher (California Library Association).

book-lover not a lady-killer, although I am told the two are not incompatible. But the point is book-*lover*. I am not here as an authority on the "great books." We are all aware of the power of certain books in influencing the course of history. Lincoln is supposed to have said when he first met Harriet Beecher Stowe: "So you are the little lady who caused this big war." And Tom Paine's *Common Sense* probably did more than any other single thing to consolidate opinion on independence and thus made the world tremble and even change its course.

But I do not wish to talk about such books as these. Rather I would like to talk about the ways in which books, that may or may not be "great," affect us all as individuals, the influence they exert upon us, and what that tells us about ourselves.

II

To begin with, books do affect us. Now and again in the perpetual struggle against censorship we run across a case in which some unattractive individual commits a particularly violent act, of rape and murder let us say, and then it turns out he has been reading horror comics, or the Marquis de Sade if he happens to be more literate than usual, or Poe's *Murders in the Rue Morgue.* Immediately a hue and cry goes up from the conservative non-reading public to the effect that this proves the case of limiting the accessibility if not preventing the publication of such books. Whereupon the liberal psychologists come forth with assurances that reading books never affected anyone. Although I am utterly opposed to censorship, I would have to disagree with the learned psychologists. You can't have it both ways. If *Common Sense* could prompt men to rally round the flag and die for their country, then it is certainly possible that reading the Marquis de Sade could stimulate someone to excessive unpleasantness in social behavior. I think it likely, of course, that no one not already predisposed to the revolutionary cause was deeply affected by *Common Sense,* but the point is that if it hadn't come along, or something very much like it, who is to say that independence would have been won?

We don't, of course, have to act upon those sentiments aroused by reading a particular book to be influenced by it. Indeed, the virtue of books in this sense is that they enable us to undergo many experiences vicariously. The process matures us because we are broadened and enriched and hence more understanding of that curious creature, man.

When I was about seven years old, I read a book called *Toby Tyler; or, Six Weeks with the Circus*, the story of a small boy who went off with a circus and had many exciting experiences, the most important of which was that he became very close friends with a monkey. Near the end of the story, in circumstances I can no longer recall, a wicked roustabout or some such person treated the monkey badly; it got pneumonia and died in Toby's arms. At that point I became so shaken with anger and grief that I could not continue reading. With tears streaming down my face, unable even to talk and shaking off my mother's importunities as to what was wrong, I left the house to let my grief subside on its own. I don't suppose it would be amiss for me to say that I probably became somewhat prepared by that little book for the cruelty one finds in the world and for the losses, too, one has to endure sooner or later in life.

Books do affect us and, in the process, educate us. The books we are especially fond of also tell us a great deal about ourselves. And if we know the favorite reading of others we can learn something about them that we might otherwise not know. I shall pass over the rumor that Zane Grey's *Riders of the Purple Sage* was Dwight Eisenhower's favorite book and go on to the more interesting report of some years back on President John F. Kennedy's favorite book, Robert Cecil's biography of Lord Melbourne.

Such a choice tells us something about how Kennedy viewed himself. Karl Meyer described this in an article in *Show* Magazine, June 1964. Here is Melbourne, defined by his biographer at 47 as "the perfect man of the world, whose manner, at once unobtrusive and accomplished, could handle the most delicate situation with light-handed mastery, and shed round every conversation an atmosphere of delightful

ease." Yet there was nothing studied or posed about him.
"On the contrary, the first thing that struck most people
meeting him was that he was surprisingly, eccentrically
natural. Abrupt and casual, he seemed to saunter through
life, swearing when he pleased, laughing when he pleased. . . .
It was his frankness that, above all, astonished." There is no
need for us to marvel at Kennedy's fascination with Cecil's
book on Melbourne. He enjoyed it because he could so easily
feel he was reading about himself—and what more interesting
subject is there than oneself?

III

The charm of books, of course, is not just that they tell us
about ourselves, but about others. In history this can be
particularly important because it is often so difficult to get
students to think of the past in human terms, to realize that
those about whom they are reading were really once alive
with all the frailties and endearing qualities that they themselves possess. Books which offer the best insight into this
realization of the human-ness of the past are the published di-
aries, journals, and letters which people in an earlier time
were always writing. Edmund Morgan's book on life in
colonial Virginia makes good use of such material, including
one of the most delightful and revealing letters, written by
Theodore Bland to his wife Patsy while he was away during
one of the colonial wars. In part this is what he wrote: "For
God's sake, my dear, when you are writing, write of nothing
but yourself, or at least exhaust that dear, ever dear subject
before you make a transition to another; tell me of your going to bed, of your rising, of the hour you breakfast, dine,
sup, visit, tell me of anything, but leave me not in doubt
about your health. . . . Fear not, my Patsy, yes you 'will
again feel your husband's lips flowing with love and affec-
tionate warmth.' Heaven never means to separate two who
love so well, so soon; and if it does, with what transport shall
we meet in heaven." I like that.

If we remember that the past had its people like these,
whose sorrows and hopes, sensitivities and weaknesses were

like our own, then history will not only come alive with meaning for us, but we are more likely to see ourselves, as their inheritors, in more reasonable perspective. And it is the book which makes this possible.

Nothing will ever really fully replace the printed word in this sense, in making possible the kind of intimacy and immediacy achieved by the recording of one's thought in private on paper at the time. Neither television nor the tape recorder permits this atmosphere of privacy, of immediacy, of setting one's own pace; for both by their very nature represent intrusions on these things.

IV

This does not mean that I am contemptuous of other means of communication and expression. It is sometimes said by the illiterate that one picture is worth a thousand words. I have yet to see the picture, or thousand pictures for that matter, which says what Lincoln said in two hundred fifty words in the Gettysburg Address. And I find it at least somewhat instructive that Marshall McLuhan, who argues that we now live in a visual age and that the day of the book is over, found it necessary to express his ideas in print.

But the point really is not that books are threatened by moving pictures, or for that matter by ones that do not move. The point is that man's life is enormously enriched as he expands his means of communication and expression, each of which strengthens the other. On the simplest level, for example, seeing *Doctor Zhivago* as a truly remarkable motion picture prompted many, including myself, to read Boris Pasternak's great and extraordinary novel. On a somewhat higher level, who would wish to say that his understanding of war and this form of man's inhumanity to man was not deepened by reading Tolstoy's *War and Peace* and seeing Goya's paintings?

In the computerized world we are rapidly entering, it will some day—and I believe in my lifetime—be possible for us to dial a call number which connects us to a vast library on tape and a machine in our home will quickly print the desired book for us. When that day comes, our range of choice in books will be excitingly enlarged over what it is today. If the price we must pay for this choice and convenience is the disappearance of the librarian, it is no reflection on librarians if I say the loss will be minor compared to the gain.

Frankly, I do not fear the future any more than I do the present as far as books are concerned. Motion pictures, tape, radio, television, records—these things have not thrust aside interest in books or the desire to learn from them.

V

One of the many superficial indictments against the young today is that they are more interested in records, or television, or whatever, than in books. I cannot take such a charge seriously. Enter a teenager's room; and, if you can get through the clothes strewn everywhere, the mess of posters, Bob Dylan records, and general accumulation of debris, what immediately catches the eye? Paperbacks, lots of them, and generally speaking of a variety and quality unheard of in my youth—and I was regarded as a voracious, extensive reader. At this point in preparing this paper, I walked into one of my daughters' rooms, and from the paperbacks there I picked the following at random to give you an idea of what I mean: *Silent Spring, The Tin Drum, Tender is the Night, Tarzan and the Lost Empire, Dr. Zhivago, The Brothers Karamazov, The Moonspinners, The Dharma Bums, The Varieites of Religious Experience, The Prophet, Fahrenheit 451, The Blue Guitar, Poems of Paul Verlaine, Cyrano de Bergerac, The Picture of Dorian Gray.*

Not all young people read a lot, nor do all their elders. Each generation has its share of the illiterate. But by and large young people read more and earlier than ever. I was once somewhat taken aback when I noticed one of my daughters, then aged ten, sitting on the living room lounge reading *Lolita*—and guests expected momentarily. Perhaps that is reading somewhat more and a trifle earlier than is either necessary or desirable. But as long as *Tarzan of the Apes* is around to serve as antidote, there is no real need for worry.

The young today in our society are more interested in ideas, values, and relationships as defined in very personal and human terms than they are in these things as defined in material and structural terms. It is in books that they find an important reinforcement for their interests. Note the kinds of books they are reading: books on love, sex, drugs, homosexuality, the Negro, the alienated, the helpless—whether it be in novels, poetry, the drama, sociological studies, or psychology. For example: *Drugs and the Mind,* Ayn Rand's *For the New Intellectual, Go Tell It on the Mountain, Toward a Psychology of Being, The Negro Revolt,* Thoreau's *Civil Disobedience,* Frankl's *Man's Search for Meaning, Demian, Psychotherapy East and West, The Love Poems of Kenneth Patchen, Loneliness* by Moustakas, *Zorba the Greek.* The subjects alone, much less the approach to them, are different from the subjects the young read about and were interested in thirty or forty years ago. And why not? The times not only are changing, as Bob Dylan says—they have changed.

Thirty years ago the books the young read told them society, not the individual, was the focal point. To tackle its ills you helped the workers organize, fought the police on the bloody picket line, went into the national or regional offices of the Agricultural Adjustment Agency, Social Security, or Department of Labor. Today the books the young read tell them that the individual, not society, is the focal point. To tackle ills you don't build organizations, you create movements and demonstrations; you don't pronounce class warfare, you preach love; you don't fight back on the picket line, you passively resist on the street; you aren't concerned about depressed corporations, you're concerned about depressed human beings; you don't go off to join the Abraham Lincoln Brigade in Spain, you protest the war in Vietnam; you don't go into the Triple A (where you become part of an efficient dedicated government team), you join the Peace Corps and go to Zambia where you operate on your own. And if you have for the time being given up completely on it all, you don't wander begging from town to town, as countless thousands of young people did in the depths of the depression, you settle down for a while in a pad in San Francisco with twenty or thirty others—and someone will provide.

VI

We read, in the deepest sense, to find explanations about ourselves, clues to the meaning of our lives, hints if not answers as to what we should commit ourselves to—all in terms of our own times, and those who do not read are by that much handicapped in the search. The interest the young have in such books as I have indicated suggests, of course, the deep intensity of their search in these tumultuous times. It is no less intense than it was in 1937, but it is focused and expressed differently.

If you want to follow, and perhaps better understand the gap in generations, you couldn't do better than to follow the reading interests of each. What the young of today will discover is that their children will have different interests. They will probably be as puzzled and perhaps disturbed by the books the young will read twenty-five years from now as we are today—particularly since they will still be trying to understand what is happening to them today.

Someone once commented on what he regarded as my morbid interest in novels about World War II, especially the fascination which the novel, *The Cross of Iron* by Willi Heinrich, seemed to have for me. Such an observation failed to recognize that the war was an intense, confusing personal experience for me, when I was very young, which had a great influence on my life and which I am still trying to understand. I think I understand it a little better after reading *The Cross of Iron*—even though that novel deals with the German experience on the Russian front and I fought my war in the distant Pacific.

May I recall here, without looking it up for accuracy, that conversation in *Zorba the Greek* between Zorba and the Boss after the deaths of the widow and Madame Hortense when Zorba says to the Boss: "Tell me about all these things, what do they mean, why do the young die, why does anybody die?" And the Boss answers, "I don't know." Zorba replies: "What do you mean you don't know, what about all those damn books? Why do you read them? If they don't tell you that, what the hell do they tell you?" The Boss says slowly: "They tell me about the perplexity, the anguish of men who can't answer questions like that."

Perhaps that is the most we can really hope for, to find in books our own anguish and perplexity. Surely in this lies one of the most important sources of human understanding—of ourselves as well as of others—and at no time more than the present have we greater need for this capacity. □

A PLEA FOR BOOKS

Jennifer Savary

This article is frankly prejudiced—in favor of books. Today, book reading is in danger of becoming a lost art. Instead of being a natural and enjoyable act like eating or sleeping, it has become something esoteric and rarified, a ritual with its own high priests and mumbo-jumbo. And yet, as Lester Asheim points out in "What Do Adults Read?," our society "is organized on the assumption of widespread literacy." "Our conduct is definitely altered, he says, by reading a traffic sign . . . while it would be difficult to show that our reading of *Moby Dick* had any effect at all." It is with reading of the *Moby Dick* type that we are concerned here.

The difference between merely deriving meaning from a series of writing symbols, as in reading a road sign or a recipe, and the reading of *Moby Dick* lies in the engagement and the liberation of the self. Dwight L. Burton says in the October 1966 issue of the *ALA Bulletin* that the real function of literature is to make us aware of ourselves. "The quest for true identity, he adds, is the ability to shake off, when necessary, the emotional censors of society and of self. This we can do through literature, and herein lies the great lure of literature."

But what is really happening? According to the tables published by Paul S. Lazarsfield and Patricia Kendall in *The*

Reprinted from *Stechert-Hafner Book News*, 22: 21-23, October 1967, by permission of the author and the publisher.

Process and Effects of Mass Communication in 1960, only 26 per cent of their sample had read one or more books during the previous month. On the other hand, 61 per cent read at least one magazine regularly. Among college students, 86 per cent read magazines regularly, but only 50 per cent had read one book or more in the previous month. The figures for high school students were 68 per cent for magazines and 27 per cent for books, while the equivalent figures for grade school students were 41 and 11 per cent. The figures themselves date from 1948, and they might be misleading because they are out of date, but they are borne out by a recent survey carried out by Dr. John P. Robinson, of the University of Michigan Survey Research Center. According to an article on this survey in the *New York Times* of April 17, 1967, one of Dr. Robinson's main findings was that people of little education rarely came in contact with any printed materials, "even those pictorial magazines for people 'who can't read'." Books come off badly in the popularity stakes among college students, but they don't even get to the starting post with some other sections of the population.

These are sobering figures, especially when one considers that the figures for books include paperbacks, which are a sort of hybrid between a book and a magazine. The paperbound book has most of the virtues of the magazine—availability and low price, for instance—and compactness as well. It is easy to buy as long as it is current, and easy to discard. There is almost no stigma attached to reading a paperback even in the most unintellectual circles. It is not "heavy." It is not "square"—or not very. It gets by. It might therefore be expected to be read as widely as a magazine, and thus to raise the percentage for book reading. If it does not do that, it must at least account for part of the total for book reading, which means that the readers of hard cover books are even fewer than would appear from the figures. This is understandable to a certain extent. The hard cover book is more expensive to buy and less handy to carry about. It is less easy to discard because of its bulk and its price, which inhibit sheer throwing away. But worst of all, it has a halo of intellectual prestige which damns it in the eyes of those who find reading difficult.

How has this situation come about? With all the emphasis there has been on libraries, on adult education, on teaching reading, it seems incredible that books should have become, not ubiquitous and natural companions, but intellectual status symbols. If he does not want to be accused of intellectual snobbery or worse, the reader would do well to hide his addiction to books. Better pot or alcohol than print.

It is true that the competition from other media is greater in the twentieth century than it has ever been before. Children watch television before they can talk. They see movies before they can say nursery rhymes or read tales. The radio is always with them. And none of these media requires the slightest intellectual effort. Children enjoy using their minds but they get relatively little opportunity to do so, partly because of the theory that everything must be "fun," but mainly because there are too many other things to do— easier things—and because they are not treated as embryo adults but as a special group, outside adult life. Could this be one of the causes of estrangement between the generations?

As it is easier to watch cowboys on television than to read about them in a book, children will watch television instead of reading, unless encouraged to do otherwise. This is not a criticism of television in itself. Some of the programs, such as the one that got CBS thrown out of South Africa and the recent coverage of the Middle East crisis, are remarkable contributions to our knowledge and awareness. But where the influence of television is bad is that it requires no effort on the part of the viewer. There is no involvement of the self. It promotes a passive and uncritical attitude, and it prevents the formation of the reading habit. And this is serious.

Why should it be serious? In *The Chance to Read,* the great English librarian Lionel McColvin says that without books, a man cannot be efficient and useful, cannot be himself and an individual, cannot be free. "Reading is a means of increasing one's interest in life, he says, of widening one's horizons, of increasing one's understanding." The enemies of

democracy, apathy and totalitarianism, he adds, can be
countered only by the spread of an active individualism and a
sense of responsibility, "which are little likely to flourish
among those who do not read books." This is perhaps the
crux of the malaise of our times. To read is to think, and we
need to think if we are to save our civilization from technoc-
racy, on the one hand, and barbarism, on the other.

Thought requires a vehicle of expression. Although
states of feeling can be communicated, and also recognized in
oneself, without words, ideas need to be clearly formulated.
And what do we have to formulate them with? The English
language, a marvelously rich and flexible instrument, but not
always a very precise one. If it is not to become blunted, de-
based and useless, those who speak it must be on the alert to
defend it against the encroachments of slovenliness and gob-
bledygook. All languages grow and change; they also decline
and deteriorate. The readers are the guardians of the language.
It is up to them to protest when the language is misused—
"pristine" for "white," for instance—and shades of meaning
disappear. They can recognize these dangers only if their ear
has been formed by extensive reading of their country's
literature.

But what does reading do that other media don't do for
those who are exposed to them? The difference lies in the
principle of active choice. What the viewer sees is dictated by
others. His range of choice is limited, not only by the small
number of channels but also by the fact that there is very
much the same stuff on all of them, except Channel 13. The
commercials invade his privacy, inquiring into his eating
habits, his bodily functions, the odor of his breath, but his
sense of decency is not outraged. He does not react, and in
these days of subliminal techniques and hidden persuaders,
this is dangerous. Amused and educated by television, children absorb what is fed to them, as it were by osmosis. They
do not choose. And that is not all. They are deprived of the
joys of physical contact with books, which means an im-
poverishment of their world. As a result, they are cut off
from the cultural heritage which is their birthright and

deprived of the means to protect themselves from invasions of privacy because they have not acquired the habit of concentration which reading brings. A reader is not open to the invasion of others because he is involved with the discovery of the self.

Again, how has this situation come about? There are many possible explanations, none of which is entirely satisfactory. The competition from other media is certainly one of them. Another is the desire for "instant culture," to be acquired without effort. (One French publisher finds this so shocking that he would not even have books manufactured so that they are easy to read in the subway. "Culture has to be earned," he says.) Still another is what might be called the mythology of reading. A mistaken theory about how to teach reading raised a hedge of difficulty round a very simple act and deprived a whole generation of its natural access to books. Even now that that particular theory has been exploded, the idea that reading is difficult still clings. Lester Asheim, for instance, calls reading "a highly developed skill" and says that "to be able to read with pleasure and ease requires continual practice, continual exercise, continual improvement of the skill." He puts his finger on one of the factors which militate against reading in our society when he says that "reading is not the mere passive acceptance of the efforts of others." If a reader is to get anything out of a book, he must put something of himself into it. That is true, but is reading a "highly developed skill" which requires "continual practice"?

Reading is a skill which has to be learned but, once learned, it should become instinctive, like walking. The evidence shows, however, that a large segment of the population never masters the skill sufficiently to make reading a pleasure. This seems to be due to two main factors, one mechanical and the other psychological. The first is that to the imperfectly taught, reading *is* difficult, and will remain so unless a determined effort is made to improve the skill. Part of the fault lies, therefore, with the techniques of teaching reading, and with the fact that a simple skill that can easily be learned by children under six has become something esoteric and difficult. This would hardly matter if reading was a natural part of the adult world of the home, from which children derive their sense of values. But if books and reading are not part of the home background, the child cannot be blamed for failing to acquire a skill which, as far as his observation goes, is not used.

Another psychological factor which does not encourage reading relates to the role of the businessman in a free enterprise society. Reading for pleasure does not fit in with the stereotype of the successful businessman. An executive interviewed in the survey carried out by *Fortune* and the Research Institute of America on "Why don't businessmen read books?"—mentioned by Lester Asheim in the article previously mentioned—said "Reading is not part of the concept of what a businessman should be doing. . . . The businessman is a man of action. Reading doesn't fit into that concept." Alas, poor businessman.

But that survey was carried out in 1954, and there are signs that the limitations of that attitude are being realized. According to A. P. Small, Professor of Literature at Eastern Montana College, Billings, Montana, many successful administrators in industry and government have become conscious of a lack in young executives. Writing in the *Montana Librarian* for January-April, 1966, he says, "Highly skilled specialists they may be, but they are without sufficient creativity or understanding of their times," which is attributed by the administrators to the "incredibly limited amount of non-technical reading these men have done." He adds, "Hence the slogan: 'Send me a man who reads'."

Thus, if the basic skill can be acquired, there is an incentive to read. The skill may be used, of course, to read only trash, or only newspapers and magazines. This is almost unavoidable for all the studies show that availability is the main factor in deciding what people will read, and there is a substantial amount of trash on the market. We must read the newspaper to keep informed, under pain of losing touch with our world. Magazines provide an immense range of articles to suit every taste, from the most scholarly to the practically illiterate. Much of lasting value is published in a magazine like the *New Yorker*. But reading newspapers and magazines is not a substitute for reading books, only an additional source of information and enjoyment. Assuming the content to be the same, why should a magazine be easier to read than a book? The same material appears easier to read in a magazine because it is chopped up into short sections instead of being all in one piece as in a book. The same effort seems less frightening when taken in small doses. The subsequent publication of the articles or stories in book form is a kind of accolade, an apotheosis, setting a seal upon the value of the material. And so the magazine reader can tell himself that he is just as much an intellectual as the fellow next door who reads books, only he is simple and democratic. He does not put on any intellectual side. Magazines are good enough for him.

And for the sake of this comforting feeling of belonging to the herd he will sacrifice many things. Unless he is a most unusual person, he will not have his magazines bound. He will therefore be unable to re-read an article that interested him, once the magazine containing it has been thrown out. Even if—miraculously—he keeps all the back numbers of his magazines, the issue he wants is sure to be missing—and, without indexes, how is he to find the article anyway? He must go to a library to find it, whereas he would only have to stretch his hand out for it if it was a book on his shelves. If it is not, the chances are that he will never re-read his article, for going to the library is an effort, and the periodicals room may be shut in the evening when he is free from work. He cannot usually borrow periodicals to read at home in any event. He is thus frustrated and soon discouraged.

What is to be done? Professor Small points the way in his article, when he says, "The man who reads in all likelihood is one who acquired the habit early in life, one who learned to love and revere books in his teens. . . . The avid reader and the intellectual, like good wine, require considerable time and care." Dr. Maurice F. Tauber, Melvil Dewey

Professor of Library Service at Columbia University, says in
Louis Round Wilson that Wilson considered knowing how to
use books a sign of maturity and efficiency. Dr. Tauber goes
on to comment, "Little wonder he wanted to begin with the
small child, so that the love and use of books would become
a lifelong habit." Here we have the crux of the matter. Making a "full man" takes time, and it is best to begin young.
The influence of the home is paramount. If there are books
about, if parents enjoy companionable reading, if books and
reading are as natural as air and breathing, Johnny will learn
to read, and he will be helped thereto by his natural curiosity
and the joy of using his mind. His intellectual curiosity can
be stifled, but it can also be stimulated. This is where the
adults round him bear a heavy responsibility. In a world of
violence living in the shadow of the atom bomb, he—like the
rest of us—needs something to hold on to. It can be found in
a feeling of connection and continuity with the past and the
future, an interpenetration with the thought and feeling of
our times. They are terrible and disturbing times. They are
also exciting and challenging. We all need to feel that we have
some part in them. In order to achieve this, we have to realize that we are a link between the past and the future. We
need to know about the past and to be open to contemporary
ideas in order to make the future possible, but we are in
danger of being cut off from our past and getting out of
touch with our present—because we don't read.

Our libraries are building up monumental collections
whose very size makes individual volumes virtually inacces-
sible. The only answer seems to be the computer, but the
computer provides information, not joy—and it is with joy as
much as knowledge that we are concerned in books. A civilized man can be defined as one whose life is intimately bound
up with and deeply affected by books. In our rootless communities and fear-torn world, that man will disappear unless
we cling to and obstinately defend our involvement with
books.   □

THE BOOM IN BOOKS

Peter J. Rosenwald

Where once we could gain strength in the knowledge that we were a small elite, isolated from that great crowd of those who had tried a book once and didn't like it, today we find we are no longer regarded as a race apart.

Young as I am, even I can remember that when a father found he had raised a son who was either too scared or too snobbish to go out into the world of trade and earn an honest fortune, the errant boy could always take up publishing books. Similarly, a bookish daughter could be hidden away in a library, that modern equivalent to a nunnery. And neither, mercy on us, would ever be heard of again.

Like it or not, that splendid isolation is gone forever. Publishing is no longer a private tea party in a New York salon. And librarians who once found time to get through a whole chapter of *Gone With The Wind,* sans interruption, now find it almost impossible to sandwich in a haiku between customers. We — the jealous protectors of the printed page — have been invaded by the public and dragged, preface first, into the real world of commerce.

But — quite surprisingly — publishers have been making their place in this land of buying and selling, merchandising and advertising. Books of odd and wondrous variety have been pouring forth into this expanding market, and

Reprinted by permission of the author from *Library Journal,* 86: 3223-3228, October 1, 1961.

publishers are even being recognized as bread winners in the family of industry. As the saying goes, "We're O.K. for Jack." We're just as much of a commodity as pig iron or corn flakes.

Not so long ago, the chance remark that you were engaged in the business of book making brought you either a two-year stretch in Sing Sing or a two-dollar bet on Jolly Roger in the third. And if your bookie used to be your tout, now he may turn out to be an editor of "kiddies' bookies."

So wide is this new interest in books that I expect — some day now — to see a television advertisement featuring some future Babe Ruth (in the locker room of course) huskily proclaiming "I read a little Santayana before every ball game. It helps to relieve the tension."

And if this seems to be appealing too much to the coffee table contingent, we can righteously answer, "Isn't it better to have books propping up someone's status rather than his furniture." Who knows? — perhaps today's Status Seeker may be tomorrow's Renaissance Man.

This recent emergence has had some other interesting effects. Tycoons have been seen entering libraries to find out what a "Random House" really is. It is even reliably reported that a leading banker recently commented to a friend — "I always knew the Doubledays were an excellent family, but I didn't realize they were in books."

Even the books themselves show signs of changing to match the mores of their new-found friends. "Non-books" are burgeoning. And we have learned that if cigarette manufacturers can tell the public that cancer can be fun, why then we can prove that the *Tropic of Cancer* is even funnier, and Henry Miller is really Walt Whitman; and besides, would you rather have your kid learn it in the gutter or at the knee of his librarian?

Of course, now that we are doing so well in the American economy, we have become candidates for planned obsolescence. There is more than a suspicion abroad that books may soon cease to be books at all and will become machines. If World Book and Grolier say it's so, it must be so — books will become teaching machines.

Apropos of that development, I hope that some of you haven't yet come across the limerick that *Current* magazine reprinted the other day. The original was found in the cafeteria of Columbia University's Teachers College, and goes like this:

> The latest report from the Dean
> In praise of the teaching machine
> Is that Oedipus Rex
> Could have learned about sex
> By himself, and not bothered the Queen.

We had better laugh now. Next year we may be indulging in mechanics' seminars.

So here we all are: popular, beloved, rich, mechanized. And there are those who claim all this has turned our giddy little heads. They can cite much evidence to prove that we're a bit mixed up about where we're going. To give just one example: No doubt many of you saw the recent ad which appeared in the *New York Times Book Review* offering to "Start your child on a sensible reading plan . . . designed to instill a lifetime love of good books and to assist him — without pressure — with school work . . ." So far the aim was commendable — but the premium for subscribing to the plan was a transistor radio.

Perhaps the headline should have read, "Every child needs a transistor radio to do their homework with . . ." The idea would have been no more confusing than the grammar.

Of course, say the critics, this is simply one more example of the fact that ours is a land of mass communication, mass education, and mass culture. The youngster doing his homework in semidarkness with the radio or television blaring at full volume is a part of the American scene.

But then, how is it that despite the distractions of radio and television, movies and hi-fi, comic books and cowboys — our nation is experiencing an unprecedented cultural and intellectual growth? It has been labeled, conservatively, a cultural explosion. You have surely felt its impact upon your library programs, just as we have felt it as publishers. The evidence is impressive.

In the last thirty years, Americans have increased their purchases of books by over 400 million dollars, so that now the figure hovers around the 600 million dollar mark. This increased interest in the owning of books is especially apparent in the juvenile field. In the decade from 1947 to 1957, sales of books for our young people increased by 400 per cent. Two billion copies of paperback books have been consumed since 1939, and that figure keeps rising at an astounding rate.

This has been an exciting time in the library field, too. There are now over 40,000 libraries in the United States constantly offering their wealth of services to the American people. And you have spent millions of dollars to keep your collections up to date and to expand your effectiveness. Only last year, according to the *American Library & Book Trade Annual,* our libraries spent over 110 million dollars on books and periodicals.

This cultural explosion isn't limited to the world of books — though that is the area where you and I feel it most sharply. In the fields of music and art, the story is the same. In the past three decades, the number of community symphony orchestras has grown from 30 to something like 160. In the same period, the sale of records has skyrocketed from 5½ million dollars to 400 million dollars. Despite rock-and-roll, classical music amounted to more than 20 per cent of the total. Fifteen million people across this great land turn from television sets, bridge, and baseball every Saturday afternoon to listen to the Metropolitan Opera's weekly broadcasts. Those of you who circulate records in your libraries will attest to the popularity of fine music.

The real intellectual has a ready answer for those statistics. He knows that what I'm bragging about is mass culture, not real culture. And mass culture is the antithesis of excellence. Says Dwight Macdonald, "Mass culture is not and never can be any good." To the high brow, according to Eric Larrabee, "Mass culture often means the quintessence of all the stuffed dolls, jukeboxes, outlandish architecture, scatological post cards, comic books, roadside pottery stands, and adenoidal singers with duck-tailed haircuts there ever were or will be."

But turn the coin over — surely these critics of mass culture, in their zeal for "class culture" in the traditional European sense, have lost sight of the tremendous upsurge of cultural activity in the U.S., good, bad, and indifferent, all mixed up. Surely all this activity has some meaning. The energy released by this explosion must be going somewhere. It might even be going up. The problem is an international one. Throughout the world, we are making an effort at overcoming illiteracy by teaching people to read. But are we giving them excellent material to be read? Are we guiding future generations into a trap which leaves them without any standards of quality? The eminent critic R. P. Blackmur has directed his thoughts to this problem and what he calls *the new illiteracy*.

> The old illiteracy was inability to read: as the old literacy involved the habit of reading. The new illiteracy represents those who have been given the tool of reading (something less than the old primary school education) without being given either the means or skill to read well or the material that ought to be read. The habit of reading in the new illiteracy is not limited to, but is everywhere supplied by, a press almost as illiterate as itself. It is in this way that opinion, instead of knowledge, has come to determine action.

Perhaps the greatest danger lies in the attitude of certain educated groups who have no faith in the ability of mass culture to produce another Da Vinci, or Plato, or Beethoven. These intellectuals are content to rail about the horror of mass culture. They seem to do nothing at all to raise the level of our national cultural activities. John Gardner, in his book on excellence, goes to the heart of the problem.

> An excellent plumber is infinitely more admirable than an incompetent philosopher. The society which scorns excellence in plumbing because plumbing is a humble activity and tolerates shoddiness in philosophy because it is an exalted activity will have neither good plumbing nor good

philosophy. Neither its pipes nor its theories will hold water.

These and other dangers of a mass culture are fairly obvious; the opportunities are less so. And perhaps it is even less obvious what all this has to do with libraries and publishing.

Just this. That new and enormously growing audience poses some tough questions for you. Is the beacon of light and learning, of literature in the good sense, being lost in the razzle-dazzle, neon-glow of the mass marketeers? Perhaps it is. Perhaps you keepers of the flame have failed to stoke the fire, to make it as bright as the lights of others who have gone after the mass audience with all the new techniques of mass marketing and mass merchandising. Fearful as it sounds, this phrase mass marketing means nothing more than making sure that millions, not thousands, of consumers of corn flakes can get them at the neighborhood grocery, and making sure every one of those consumers is aware that the corn flakes are there. No one need apologize for making books easy to come by for millions, and for encouraging millions to read them.

If there are not enough book stores — and we all know there aren't — then Plato reads just as well if you buy him in a drugstore. And if you buy him there because the book was in a revolving rack right under your nose as you paid for your cigarettes — then maybe there should be more revolving racks, in libraries as well as drugstores, in school hallways as well as in their libraries' tightly packed stacks. Exposure helps, as all designers of paperback jackets seem to know.

Not so incidentally, let's make all the cracks we want about the vulgarity of many paperback jackets and subjects — and let's study why they work, while we're at it.

It is easy to forget that all of us today live in a *visual* world. We have, since birth, been exposed to sound and picture every bit as much as our parents were exposed to the written word. Small wonder that our demands for visual presentation of material come naturally — just as we word-types learned from our elders to be suspicious of these devices for mass communication. Yet, note that our culture has grown and matured, not despite these mass media, but in conjunction with them.

And that brings us, the long way 'round, to books with pictures in them. If a good book has pictures in it, it is not necessarily a less good book. It is probably a better book. And if a book's subject almost demands illustration, and its pictures are made an integral part of the narrative, then it's probably better yet. And if the pictures are well reproduced, and big enough to see, and laid out to appeal to the eye — then you have a remarkably fine book.

Also an expensive book. But I see no reason why a nation which can and does pay more than is absolutely minimal for its cars, its baseballs, its toys, its weddings, and even its basic, cellophane-wrapped foods should not also be able to pay for a better cultural package — and that goes for our books and also for the facades, the furniture, and the salaries in your libraries.

There is little reason to have a battle for the badge of cultural merit between advocates of pictures and advocates of words. Sure, it is hard for some who love nothing better than the smell and feel of old books to admit that — "it isn't holy just because it's writ." On the other hand, it's a poor cliché to say that a picture is worth a thousand words. We know this is not true. Yet some pictures are priceless, and no words, no matter how well put down, can convey the impression of the visual image.

The new wave of publishing — mass produced, visually exciting books and magazines, produced and merchandised for maximum distribution — is coming of age. Modern techniques which permit the reproduction of all kinds of illustrated material — from a Skira art book to a recent and thorough photographic study of Brigitte Bardot — have tremendous potential for good and for evil.

But I would like to nourish the thought that quite a lot of these modern books and magazines — the ones that combine the best of journalism with the best of illustration — deserve to be accepted as a legitimate and worthy branch of literature, in the best sense of that emotion-laden word.

Of course, it is not the form, but the degree of excellence of the content, that will determine any book's ultimate value as literature. Excellence of content, let us hope, will always be far more important than the quality of the binding, the paper, or another material factor. The sturdiest binding adds little to a poor book. A great work will achieve its place without buckram or an extra super-strength binding, but such factors do not eliminate form as an essential part of books and literature. You don't see many people reading scrolls nowadays.

NEW BREED OF EDITORS
But, I would like to suggest that a new breed of editors and wtiters — the picture journalists — offers our young friend before the television set and the more conservative reading public a new tool for learning and for cultural enjoyment. We are perplexed by the paradox of the love of good books and of the transistor radio, partly because we forget what the literary diet of earlier generations was actually like. Go back to the Frank Merriwell stories and the dime novels if you want to find an equivalent to today's radio and television fare. Despite the fact that dime novels were smuggled into composition books 50 years ago, our parents and our grandparents managed to find time to read good books too and grow up relatively unharmed. The only differences were in the "medium."

To get back to mass marketing, there's obviously a lot more to it than an attractively designed, well-engineered product.

Given that, we have to stop the consumer in his tracks and make him buy our books, our product, to the exclusion of some other product or diversion. What's to arrest our smoking man and make him a thinking man? The answer, as we all know, but sometimes hate to admit, is advertising and promotion.

Now those two words, advertising and promotion, have gotten themselves a pretty shoddy reputation of late, but they needn't offend. While some advertisers have irritated us all to the point that we have constructed our own handy invisible shield, giving us twenty-four hour protection from the advertiser, others have charmed us into awareness of products and services which we might have missed.

Imaginative advertising, promotion, and distribution — hard, unpleasant, commercial-sounding words — account as much for the success of our magazines and books as do their artistic accomplishments. The public was there. We at American Heritage went after them to capture some of their leisure time and money. We promoted the product diligently, and, I believe I can honestly say, without insulting the intelligence of our audience or finding the lowest common denominator. Several other publishers of fine books and magazines are doing as well or better. Through editorial, production, and marketing devices and a good deal of luck, we have found a way to provide good products which fit within the framework of the cultural explosion and to capture the imagination of the public long enough to get them to stop, look, and, hopefully, to read.

Sure, it's startling to see a radio used to entice people to try books. But just think of the number of discount stores which have recently taken to offering books at tremendously reduced prices as a come-on for all sorts of merchandise — including transistor radios. Books are used in supermarkets and in drugstores as "loss leaders," attractive bargains to bring the consumer into the store.

The implication is exciting. If quality books can be merchandised in the same way as other products, there is an ever-growing market for them. What an outrage it is, really, that a best seller in the U.S. often means that the book has sold only 20,000 copies. It need not be so.

Those of us who love to spend time with books must realize that the days of browsing in bookstores are over. The commercial realities make it harder and harder for bookstores to encourage the shopper to taste the delights of a page here, a paragraph there. Only the library offers the opportunity for bibliographic gastronomy. And yet, to compete with the blare of the television and other distractions, the libraries have had to raise their voices to remind the public of their existence. They have had to offer new services in new ways.

And sometimes they have had to abandon ultra-conservatism in favor of new policies.

Libraries throughout the land are, like publishers, realizing the advantages of policies and programs designed to capture the interest and attention of today's busy citizen. Librarians are to be lauded for their unselfish efforts to maintain a standard of excellence, to see to it that the great works of literature remain readily available to the reader even where publishers and booksellers could not afford to keep them in print. Think of the hundreds of books which have been revived in popularity through their constant availability in libraries and through the quiet counsel of librarians.

And yet, librarians are often called the underpaid custodians of the morgues of culture. It is a deplorable fact that all too often, libraries have, through unwillingness to recognize new trends, lost out to other media in receiving their share of attention.

CULTURE'S DISCOUNT HOUSES

You will forgive me, I hope, if I suggest that libraries are culture's discount houses and that they would do well to look upon the cultural explosion much as the discount store looks on the economic scene. Libraries offer the greatest cultural bargains available. On their shelves can be found a variety of experiences matched nowhere else. There is a host of cultural consumers out there, and they are going to spend their time indulging their desire for intellectual activity. Maybe it will be at the movies or in front of the TV set or watching Rome burn. But with your superb competitive advantage, it *can* be with fine books and services supplied by your libraries.

You have to arrest their attention, not their persons (like librarian Harold Roth in New Jersey) but you do have to catch their interest. And no one is in a better position to do it than the library.

When I told one of our copy writers about this paper, he said that to write a direct-mail letter for a library would be a copy writer's dream. He is used to penning phrases like, "Send no money — we will bill you later," or "Try this issue

FREE." So, let's suppose that you were to decide on a direct-mail campaign to the people in your community — a letter designed, quite frankly, to sell them the idea of using the library. What would you say — how would you convert your library into a discount house of culture? Here's what our copy writer's dream letter sounded like.

DEAR FRIEND:
 This is to inform you that we owe you a refund on your taxes. You and the other members of the community have paid X dollars a year for the use of your library — and you haven't come in to collect your share.
 Your refund, according to our books, comes to FREE use of 148,971 different titles. As a special this week, we are offering the complete works of Mark Twain, the writings of Henry James, the masterpieces of Dumas, and 21 free look-ups of *any word you want to say* in Webster's handy dictionary.
 And that's not all. During this BIG CLEAR-THE-BOOKS WEEK, if you will promise 15 minutes of your time via the enclosed postage-paid reply card, we shall give you *in addition:*

 1) An exhibit of Civil War prints,
 2) A recorded chamber music concert in the garden behind the library,
 3) A truly wonderful professional to entrance your kids with readings from non-beat, and often off-beat, works of poetry and prose any Saturday morning in the children's section, and
 4) All the records you can borrow in 10 minutes' frenzied picking!

 Bring the family, for some special "togetherness" surprises — *see for yourselves,* in the privacy of your own home, how READING ALOUD can keep you all out of the refrigerator for hours on end!
 But act now! Remember, paper deteriorates, and all our books are made of it. Get *your* books before they're gone or crumby. Look smart, *be* smart. See me in the stacks. I'll be expecting you. . . .
       (signed) Your friendly librarian

P.S. We're open all day, every day, and on weekends as well — and it's all FREE. And remember, a family that reads, succeeds!

BOOKS IN THE COMPUTER AGE

William Ready

There is something in the earth that makes a nation. It is, for example, the soil of France which forms the soul of it, so that were all the present French to pass away and a new barbarous people inhabit the land, speaking Tartar or a clicking African tongue, German even, or Australian, within a generation or so those people would grow French, and shrug and save, as like as any Frenchman of today.

The people who chaffe in the market places of Athens are very different in appearance from those ancient Greeks who drove their bargains there, but as Gerald Durrell says, Aristophanes would find them just the same grist for the mill of his humor.

Likewise, in every American north of the Rio Grande, there is Yankee. Yankee know-how has survived and taken root, seeded and flourished in every wave of migration that has flooded over the original nutmeg swindles of Connecticut, and the gin mills of Eli Whitney. Americans are happier tinkering with a gadget than with any true exercise of the mind, like reading. Even their writing has a tinkering quality about it, a preoccupation with the way things work out, be they live or mechanical.

American librarians would much rather switch-on than read, turn a screw rather than a page. They have been turned-

Reprinted from *Stechert-Hafner Book News*, 24: 17-18, October 1969, by permission of the author and the publisher.

on by the glitter, the whir, and the shine of the new machines and the electronic devices that they think will save the libraries for them by doing away with the books therein. Administrators welcome the new library computer age also, having been assured that it will relieve them of the burden of supporting the vast numbers of books that accumulate within learned libraries, without, it seems ever being read at all, or circulated in any way that can form a statistic that will enable them to increase their grant from the provincial or state legislatures.

Computer Science is becoming a must course in the library schools. They are being deaned more and more by engineers of this new and surprising method of controlling learning; the practising librarians love it. They never have time to read books anyhow; they regard as suspect, as a poseur, an odd body, anyone of their ancient craft who claims to read. Let any librarian write lovingly about books that he has read or wishes to read and the professional library magazines will denounce him more violently than they would some library trustee who had removed *Tropic of Cancer* from a high school library. Their journals are full of information about anything but books, save how to buy and process them.

Recently a university president was showing off his new complex of buildings. . . . How university administrators love their buildings! They are worse than parish priests; they suffer from the same Edifice Complex. When it was remarked that the library book stock was meagre and small in relation to the language-arts laboratory or his science-research centre, his pools and auditoriums, he chirped back cheerfully that that was all right; it was all intended. He pointed to a plug in the wall and mentioned that the plug was better, because from it he could pipe in all the millions of books in the world, to be played on a console which was like a baby Wurlitzer. There are people who really believe this, besides the rascals who know better. They look forward to the day when, lying on a divan, they can read the *Purgatorio* with Dali illustrations projected on the ceiling, and drop off to sleep on a mattress wired for nocturnal learning, so that they

will awake in the morning all fed in the mind with the Second
Law of Thermodynamics or the contradictory criticism of
F. R. Leavis; even a judgment value will have been transmitted into them which will depend on the whim or creed of a
programmer who died last week—an accident with a
computer.

Eyes light up, cheeks flush, tongues are loosened, an air
of light pervades some library professional meetings now as
never before, because the participants have been freed from
the shadow of the guilt that haunted them in those B.C. days
when they were supposed to care for books. Now they are
engaged in a vast confidence game with the salesmen of the
machines, with the administrators who believe that their institutions can now do without a library, with the education-
ists who are daft on resource centres that do not contain a
book but only ephemera at the best, and are filled instead
with films, records, Xerox copies of information that, in
many cases, is better and more conveniently, and far more
cheaply available in a book.

Now this is not to denigrate the use of the machine. We
are living in an age of technology. But we will be doing our
own kind and the Machine a disservice if we yield to that,
when all of the learning and the wisdom that we amassed
from the times past, present and to come, are contained within the covers of a book.

Human actions are now conditioned by the Machine.
Things are not done because the machines shy from them.
Demolition of the past comes easy with the power of this
assembled force. Out of the dust of the ruins a modern
Sauron, who begins as a Man and becomes a Board of Control, can conjure up visions of Man's future where there is no
bloody sweat, no tears; all will be accomplished for Man's
pleasure with the lift of a finger, the blink of an eye, but at
the cost of the deliverance of his future to the Board, computer-oriented Board, clean and shining Board, powerful
beyond-all-the-measures-of-ordinary-Man Board. If Sauron
has his way, there will be only one Board, and it's mustering,
not in the shady cover of Mirkwood, but in carpeted, un-
bugged or bugged conference rooms. . . .

Computers can be the best friends that libraries will ever have. Resource centres can further enrich the scope, depth and treasure of our libraries because film is Book, discs are Book, so are slides and magnetic tapes. They serve well and often for the future that began at Gutenberg. Indeed, in order to control the plethora of information, in order to produce a new right form, even of the Book, we will need to use all the new technological aids. Moreover in the most academic of libraries, even in Bodley's or at Cambridge, the computer is beginning to play its part as an aid in getting some sort of order out of the library administration, service and acquisition. MARC, Shared Cataloguing, order forms that cannot be sent, pierced or spindled, all can gradually increase the efficiency of library service. But the library must and will remain Book to the core, if it is to withstand the vulgar enthusiasms and the silly terms of those who think of it as passé.

More and more academic libraries with the covert or overt wish as may be, and with the hopeful anticipation of the administration, faculty and students, are putting more and more of their budget into controlling and programming what they don't have enough of, the Book. No library can ever have enough Book, and all these means bring libraries closer to sharing their resources: but it must be Fair Share.

Groucho Marx once remarked with pleasure upon Beppo's statement that to have a football team you need football players. The sense of this cannot be denied, any more than the statement that you cannot have a library as a resource unless you have books. Academic libraries' budgets all over North America show a diminution in the amount of money spent for books, offset by the greater proportion of the budget spent for technological aids to control the relatively dwindling mass of them.

Library schools are turning out more and more computer-oriented students, impatient experts. Librarians are courting them in a way that they never court bookmen, unless they buy the book shop and the bookseller goes along with it, or a great collection with its curator.

Beware, lest we neglect the major for the less. It will be

a long time, perhaps never, before anything so convenient, so compact, so portable, so possible to steal, hide and print in a small, poor place, will be discovered that will better the Book. Above all there is a danger to Freedom, that first essential quality of a university, if we depend upon one of the great technological centres for our information, or data, or synthesis, or retrieval, rather than upon books, which are harder to destroy than any film, any tape, any central reservoir of information data on discs. Moreover books can be passed around, even if need be, surreptitiously, whenever freedom is threatened. A hand press, as Resistance and Underground history shows, can do more harm to Sauron than bullets or barricades. After all, it is a battle for the minds of men that we are involved in, and books remain our surest ammunition, our basic ration for the mind that is under fire.

Books are going up in price and they will cost more next year than they cost now, but every transaction that is greeted with a wild huzza, whereby pages are sent through the electronic media, cost generally far more than the price of the book in the first place. Acquisition of book and related materials should remain the prime concern of academic libraries and all else should be ancillary, including the desires and dreams of the librarians who would be happy to be Yankee and not Brahmin. □

Learn with BOOK

R. J. Heathorn

A new aid to rapid—almost magical—learning has made its appearance. Indications are that if it catches on all the electronic gadgets will be so much junk.

The new device is known as Built-in Orderly Organised Knowledge. The makers generally call it by its initials, BOOK.

Many advantages are claimed over the old-style learning and teaching aids on which most people are brought up nowadays. It has no wires, no electric circuit to break down. No connection is needed to an electricity power point. It is made entirely without mechanical parts to go wrong or need replacement.

Anyone can use BOOK, even children, and it fits comfortably into the hands. It can be conveniently used sitting in an armchair by the fire.

How does this revolutionary, unbelievably easy invention work? Basically BOOK consists only of a large number of paper sheets. These may run to hundreds where BOOK covers a lengthy programme of information. Each sheet bears a number in sequence, so that the sheets cannot be used in the wrong order.

To make it even easier for the user to keep the sheets in the proper order they are held firmly in place by a special locking device called a "binding."

Reprinted from *Punch*, May 9, 1962, p. 712, by permission of the Ben Roth Agency, Inc., Scarsdale, New York. © *Punch* 1962.

Each sheet of paper presents the user with an information sequence in the form of symbols, which he absorbs optically for automatic registration on the brain. When one sheet has been assimilated a flick of the finger turns it over and further information is found on the other side.

By using both sides of each sheet in this way a great economy is effected, thus reducing both the size and cost of BOOK. No buttons need to be pressed to move from one sheet to another, to open or close BOOK, or to start it working.

BOOK may be taken up at any time and used by merely opening it. Instantly it is ready for use. Nothing has to be connected up or switched on. The user may turn at will to any sheet, going backwards or forwards as he pleases. A sheet is provided near the beginning as a location finder for any required information sequence.

A small accessory, available at trifling extra cost, is the BOOKmark. This enables the user to pick up his programme where he left off on the previous learning session. BOOKmark is versatile and may be used in any BOOK.

The initial cost varies with the size and subject matter. Already a vast range of BOOKS is available, covering every conceivable subject and adjusted to different levels of aptitude. One BOOK, small enough to be held in the hands, may contain an entire learning schedule.

Once purchased, BOOK requires no further upkeep cost; no batteries or wires are needed, since the motive power, thanks to an ingenious device patented by the makers, is supplied by the brain of the user.

BOOKS may be stored on handy shelves and for ease of reference the programme schedule is normally indicated on the back of the binding.

Altogether the Built-in Orderly Organised Knowledge seems to have great advantages with no drawbacks. We predict a big future for it.   □

BOOKS IN A COMMUNICATIVE ENVIRONMENT

Ilo Fisher

This is a reading world. Despite the impact of radio and television a larger percentage of our population is reading today
than ever before in our history. While it seems unlikely that
radio and television are going to put bookstores or magazine
stands out of business, it has not been clearly established that
reading in libraries is flourishing proportionately. Many readers seem to prefer purchasing numbers of paperback books at
the news-stand to obtaining them free of charge at the local
library. Why?

Examine the titles of books offered by the bookstore.
Many of them are light romances and westerns, to be sure.
But look more closely. There are an increasing number of
classical titles. Even in 1953, *The Pocket Book of Verse* containing great poems of England and America sold over a million and a half copies. In 1959 we are talking of the "higher
priced paperbacks" and "paperback originals". One would
hardly quarrel with the quality of such titles as *Three Great
Plays of Euripides, Roget's Pocket Thesaurus, A Dictionary
of English Literature,* or *A Guide to the Religions of America.*
All of these are good library titles to be found in even the
smallest library. Why then, do people buy rather than borrow
that to which they are entitled?

Perhaps it is the place in which they plan to read these

Reprinted from *The Rub-Off*, 10: [2-5], March-April, 1959, by permission of the author and the publisher, J. George Ort.

books. Many of the best paying news-stands are located in
busy train stations, and bus depots. Much of the reading of
the present day busy American is done while he is going to
and from work. Usually he does not have time to sit in the
library and read. His days off must be crowded with other
mundane affairs. He could borrow the book, however, from
the local library and carry it with him, just as he is carrying
his paperback volume.

Maybe, as our reader selects his book at the department
store or corner bookstore, he plans to take home where he
can put on casual clothes and be comfortable. What is wrong
with a short trip to the local library to bring home several
well chosen titles for leisure reading in the same casual, comfortable atmosphere? Obviously, personal reading habits play
a large part in readers' book selection and this selection can
be vital to libraries and librarians.

People read for many reasons. In their early years it is
usually to fulfill some assignment. In their middle and later
years it is usually to extend the knowledge acquired in those
earlier assignments, but they read also for other reasons: information, insight, understanding, enjoyment, and escape.
Reading is a personal experience. Books can be picked up or
laid down at will. They can be read rapidly or slowly, in parts
or as wholes. They can be pondered upon or devoured without question. What the reader selectes to read for his own enlightenment or enjoyment is certainly not what someone else
may select for him to read. But he can be encouraged to
select and read titles he may not have considered on his own
initiative.

What influences the reader's selection in the first place?
It may be previous knowledge of the author — an old friend.
It may be knowledge of the subject. He may be influenced by
the fact that the title is on the best seller list or has been
strongly recommended by a business acquaintance. It could
be that the reader is trying to add to his store of information
and is reading systematically. Assuming it is none of these
and that he is just trying to find something which strikes his
fancy, what aspects of the bookstore or news-stand would

draw him closer to books than the local library would draw him?

Non-verbal communication, or more simply, the language of objects, is boldly used in the world of trade. Here store windows and commercial displays are arranged with the recognized purpose of attracting buyers. Displays mean dollars and cents to the merchant. Has the librarian attacked the problem with the same intensity?

The effects that books as objects achieve in communicative value are dependent not only on arrangement, shape, size, and material, but also upon environment. Paperbacks, for example, beg to be taken for reading on the commuters' train. They are soft, pliable, informal and seem to be made to fit into purse or pocket. The same is more or less true of magazines. Hard bound books, on the other hand, are stiff and formal, conveying finality of selection. They are durable and they show it.

Book designers, along with retail advertisers in all fields, have long made use of non-verbal communication in design and composition. Merchants take advantage of the artistry of the book jacket, using it as the center of effective posters, displays, and arrangements. Many librarians do too, but there are those who discard all book jackets, preferring to emphasize utility, efficiency, and durability. What opportunities they miss to invite customers to examine their book collections!

Many copies of the same title in attractive dust jackets do not detract from a shelf of books; on the contrary, they make the books very tempting. Seven copies of *Peter Rabbit* illustrated with the exquisite drawings of Beatrix Potter delight the heart at any age. On the other hand, seven copies of the *Works of Dickens* in black, tan, or gray deaden a shelf of books, no matter how interesting the subject matter between those drab covers may be. With the latter, certainly the ideas of plentiful supply and ready availability are communicated, but something even stronger takes precedence — something long lasting and not altogether pleasant.

What about color? Primarily, the realm of the artist?

Granted. But is it true that color makes the everyday life of the average citizen tolerable or intolerable? Does the merchant not use color advantageously at every opportunity? Is there any good reason why a library should not sparkle with color?

Vivid in my mind is a visit, some years ago, to a high school library in one of our large cities. Woodwork, desks, tables, and floor were of the customary dark wood. The library shelves, though made of the same dark wood, were bright with light blue buckram bindings. The effect was good — if you like light blue buckram — I do. Recently, a book salesman confided that he could always sell books to one of his customers, if the books had blue covers. Blue, assuredly, has its place in book covers and in the realm of personal choice of the librarian. I can imagine, however, that there are library patrons who do not like blue at all — "blue is such a cold color".

Have we given much thought to the communicative value of texture and design in the paper and cloth used in the book trade? These materials convey subtleties which the literal meanings of words are quite incapable of expressing. Have you ever watched a woman shop for dress material? Invariably, she rubs it between her fingers. Smoothness, roughness, stiffness, lightness, coldness, warmth — all have immediate meaning for her, yet she reads no label. No clerk discourses on the fine qualities of the material. Indeed, the latter, to whom the customer sometimes pays little heed, may be of no use except to ring up the sale. The shopper buys what pleases her or she does not buy at all. Though she may not do it as deliberately, she shops for a book with the same notions in mind: testing the quality of the cloth covers, considering the elegance of the paper and the appropriateness of the type face, weighing them against what appears to be the contents. If it pleases her or meets her need, she considers further; if it displeases her, or excites no interest, she lays it down.

Surfaces, too, have their messages. Aged vellum, for example, speaks loudly of an old, perhaps, rare book. Surfaces express mood. The roughly textured cloth with its hand-somely embossed design which covers a new book on daggers, swords, and small weapons appropriately suggests rugged and violent living. The leather strap with its minutely carved bronze dagger fastener is the epitome of all the book stands for. One would hardly expect to find the same kind of sur-face or lock on a Bible.

We need to capture the messages these everyday materi-als are sending. Consciously or unconsciously, they are read-ily understood by all, though they may not always be used to their fullest. Librarians, in particular, need to take stock of them. Displays, bookshelves, and furnishings must excite more attractive messages. Most of all, books themselves must be arranged with the recognized purpose of attracting patrons. Just as clearly as the church building with all its furnishings indicates to the observer in some way the nature of the ser-vices inside, the library building in its entirety must transmit, to the best of the librarian's ability, the nature of the library service offered.   □

THOUGHTS ON BOOKS AND LIBRARIES

Edwin Wolf 2nd

A consultant in communication arts recently stated, "I maintain that the book is an archaic method of storing information." I disagree—emphastically! I like books, those four-square objects that you can hold in your hand. I like old books, the feel of them, the smell of them, the way they're printed, even the idea of them. I like the people who work with them, know them, care for them, collect them. I don't like microfilms, magnetic tapes, computer cards, technical experts in librarianship, or the idea of information retrieval by machines. This puts me in the species, according to Linnaean terminology, of *dinosaurus bibliothecarius,* an implication that my kind of bumbling, humanistic approach to libraries and scholarship is doomed to extinction. The brave new world will have no place for a librarian who is a square when it comes to non-book books. I am happy that I live on the fringe of change, so that I can probably hang on, at least as a specimen of what used to be, until a book mechanic takes my place. I can only hope that my fossil remains may stir some interest a generation or two in the future.

Having served an apprenticeship of twenty years in the rare-book business as the boy in the back-room who compiled catalogues and attended to bibliographical details, I am a firm believer in discipline, at least, in scholarly discipline. I learned by learning, not by pushing buttons. Thanks to the nature of the Rosenbach business, I saw, handled, and worked with a vast variety of old books and manuscripts. And this is exactly the way most of us acquired our knowledge, our understanding, and our love of books. I have little patience with the bright young man who comes into a library seeking "original" material on which to work, and is so little saturated with the subject under consideration that he expects the library to make a transcription of an eighteenth-century document because he has never learned to read a hand which, as it is all too frequently put, uses f's instead of s's.

As I see the problem, it is not whether or not a research institution, a rare-book library, provides help for someone who uses it. Of course, we do. We provide catalogues, good, bad, and indifferent. Most of us try to supplement what appears on those cards from our personal knowledge of the collection in our custody, and we have reference books and bibliographies to supplement the catalogue and our knowledge. Given a topic, we can usually help the seeker up the front steps and inside the door. But if a student of sixteenth-century English literature has never heard of the STC, the vast, book-by-book accumulated knowledge of a Jackson about such books will be too rich to digest. If a student of colonial American history has never heard of Evans, Shipton's deep, personal familiarity with early American printed books will be over his head. It is amazing to me how much information is available in already published indexes and bibliographies, what a tremendous amount is in the brains of the experts, and how little of it is known to the push-button boys.

No index is better than the person who made it. There are good bibliographies and bad bibliographies, but "a bibliography" is nothing magic. In some cases the best that can be said about it is that it's better than nothing, and the worst that someone other than its compiler should have done the job. It's the better than nothing approach that I resent, and this seems to me the approach of the gadgeteers and the automatic information retrievers.

If we could put the title of every book ever printed into a computer with a subject index built in, then, theoretically, anyone could get out of it a complete subject-catalogue. Yet, it would be no better than the knowledge of the subject-cataloguers who fed the information into the machine. I don't think there is a computer-indexer in the world who would be much help to any of us in our own fields, unless he knew more than we do.

Isn't it that unusual bit of information which we have and which the other fellow missed that makes the book game an adventure and not a chore?

You wouldn't be able to tell from what I've written so far, but I love indexes. (I only use the word "indices" in things like Library Company annual reports.) I love bibliographies. I even write them. Every day I sing a silent hymn to the memory of a patient soul whose life-work makes my day's work easier. One of my problems as a librarian is that too few people who come a-researching know about these patient souls and their works. One of the great problems of teaching is not to pump a student full of information, but to teach him how to extract further information. Surely, more important than knowing a fact is knowing where to find that fact. I don't think that can be automated.

Sometimes I don't know which side I'm on. At the moment I wish indexers had indexed colonial Philadelphia like mad. I am suffering the frustration of trying to identify John Doe or Richard Roe who left a collection of books in his estate of sufficient interest for me to want to know a little about him, a thumb-nail-sketch's worth. If I'm lucky someone once mentioned his name in an article in the *Pennsylvania Magazine of History* and its index leads me to him. If I'm not lucky and if he's not in the *Colonial Archives* or the genealogies of Keith's *Provincial Councillors of Pennsylvania,* and if he's not a lawyer, so that he's not in Martin's *Bench and Bar in Philadelphia,* and if he's not a known cabinetmaker or silversmith, and if he's not in a number of obvious reference works, and if I've found his will and am not interested in his land transactions, I'm just about through.

But everything I may want to know—and more—may be sitting on a few pages of the *Pennsylvania Gazette* or the *Pennsylvania Journal*. Sometimes, when it's important and I'm both desperate and not too busy, I go hunting needles in newspapers.

If Philadelphia colonial newspapers were indexed the way the *Virginia Gazette* is, I would lose some of the most fascinating and most productive hours I spend. If we had all newspapers so well indexed that no one would have to peregrinate through them in search of his own grail, we would not pick up those juicy tidbits of information which go into the saddlebags of our memory. For the present, all you may have wanted was a fact, but for the future you acquired a feeling for the times. I wonder how many people do what is generally called "wasting time" by leafing through the *Virginia Gazette* these days. I wonder how many people leaf through, or roll through, any microfilms, hailed by the crew of library mechanics not only as substitutes for books, manuscripts, and periodicals but better than the originals.

I cannot accept microfilms or microcards or magnetic tapes as a substitute for the original. As expedients for the inexpensive transmission of texts from a library to a scholar's desk, miles apart, for circumscribed use, these gadgets of reproduction are wonderful. But we are being assailed by a barrage of hard salesmanship, which tells us not to bother about the expense of the real thing; just get it microfilmed. This attack on the rare book and the autograph document has put us antiquarians on the defensive. We are in the position of having to justify what has survived and been hymned for centuries. It's time to counterattack.

My intention is not to talk of the aesthetics, the aura, the feeling of the writer and his times which is inherent in an original. Bookmen from Richard de Bury to Robert Taylor have done that better than I can. No. I have something shocking to tell. It is now being rumored around that some microfilms have deteriorated to the point of illegibility, and that some magnetic tapes have scrambled to the point of unintelligibility. The enthusiasts, or most of them, have been so excited about the advantages of their systems that they forgot to ask a very basic question: how permanent are they? We now know scientifically—thanks to Mr. Barrow of Richmond—what makes paper last, how long it will last, and what to do to make it last. No one has bothered to ask the same things about these new-fangled keepers of records. If you spend hundreds of thousands of dollars putting information into a computer, are you told how long that information will be available?

When I began writing this, all I had heard were rumors. Very recently a kind friend in Washington sent me a release from the National Bureau of Standards, dated 25 Sept. 1963, headed, "Microscopic Defects in Film." In conservative, low-keyed fashion it says that for a year the Bureau has been studying defects which appear on microfilm negatives from two to twenty years old. Thousands of rolls of microfilmed government records, the release goes on, have been inspected, "and a widespread incidence of defects noted." Nothing has yet been lost, the report assures us; this is not what gossips told me. The defects are known as "J-type defects," and research will continue. The rumors which reached me before this statement was released were considerably more lurid. A major archive which had filmed and destroyed originals was panicking internally and assuring the world that all was well. The largest single consumer and user of microfilms was experiencing trouble, as it was mildly put.

Let me go on with the chronicle of whispered, but unsubstantiated, horrors. I've been collecting them. A municipality photostated all its property records, kept only the negatives for use, and microfilmed them for security; the original records were destroyed. (Saves space, you know.) The photostats are now beginning to go brittle, and no legible print can be made from the film. A radio station made special orchestral recordings for its own use. Within two years the independent magnetic fields set up in the coiled tape, as I was told, had so scrambled the recordings that they were useless. Some while ago a record company is reported to have put all its master discs on tape and thrown away the discs. (Saves space, you know.) Now, the tapes cannot be used to make new records. What about those supposedly permanent archives of recorded history?

I want to be very careful to say that there may not be anything inherently wrong with microfilms or tapes; the trouble may well be in the way some particular films or tapes were processed or stored. For example, do you know any library or archive which tests a roll of film for acidity? I know one, the Eleutherian Mills Historical Library. Yet, we know that it is the acid in paper which causes it to deteriorate, and we are now talking about de-acidification of paper to restore its permanence/durability. It is perfectly possible that the films which are deteriorating are only those which were carelessly washed when they were developed and retained acids on their surfaces. Do you know any major user of microfilms who has been concerned about the processing? We do know that after a certain amount of use a film becomes scratched to the point of poor image. Has there been inaugurated a regular program to replace such film from the negative, or to make sure that the negative itself is in good condition?

Twenty some years ago the Historical Society of Pennsylvania microfilmed the *Pennsylvania Gazette*. This year, because the old negative, after being used for a large number of positives, was not in first-class condition and because improvements in microphotography have been so great as to permit a far better image, the Society has refilmed the *Gazette*. The libraries which bought the original film have had more than their money's worth in time and transportation costs saved for their readers. My point is not that the film was, and is, worthless. It served its purpose. Fortunately, the only runs of the *Gazette* which are complete are the sets in the Historical Society and the Library Company and they are still in existence, and can be filmed, if necessary, two decades from now. A large sum of money was made available for the filming of the *Philadelphia Inquirer* from the beginning. Once again the only two sets which could make the project possible were in the Historical Society and the Library Company, but we were told that the volumes would

have to be guillotined to be adequately photographed because they were big and tightly bound. For the years of the
sulphite period they could not be rebound, because of the
extreme brittleness of the paper. In other words, the runs
would be destroyed. We thought long and hard and decided
not to permit it. We were called stuffy.

Now I am told that we were so conservative that we
were farsighted. A new method of spray de-acidification, no
more expensive than, but just as expensive as, microfilming,
may prove feasible. It may enable us to save the crumbling
sulphite-impregnated pages of the past century of cheap pulp
newspapers, and we will not be forced to rely upon the ques-
tionable crutch of film for preservation. But what would have
happened if our runs of the *Inquirer* were no more and the
negative film developed the J-type defect?

I admit to being old-fashioned. I am proud to be the
custodian of books and manuscripts which somehow or other
did survive in a library now 232 years old. You all are the
owners, custodians, or lovers of similar artifacts containing
the written or printed word which are like marvels of preservation. We are accustomed to think in terms of centuries. It
seems to me that our responsibility for keeping the links of
this physical cultural chain with the past unbroken is as great
as that of making the chain useful. I am continually reminded
that eminent scholars did work with the resources of libraries
in what I may term the Dark Ages of poor lighting, inadequate heating in winter, no air-conditioning in summer, im-
perfect or nonexistent catalogues, and ink in bottles on reading desks, and those eminent scholars wrote books of distinction. Today we could give those same scholars more information more quickly and enable them to work more comfortably; yet the books they wrote are qualitatively as good as
the author was a researcher and the researcher was an author.
I do not think all the films or cards or tapes, while they may
be of assistance to a mature mind, can make a bad scholar
good or a bad book acceptable. I firmly believe that no
machine can be a substitute for a good bookman and I firmly
believe that there is no substitute for the original printed or
written word on paper or vellum. Have you ever heard of anyone who read a microfilm for pleasure?   □

GREAT LAND OF LIBRARIES

Lawrence Clark Powell

I could broach my subject, Great Land of Libraries, as
Melville broached *Moby Dick*—remember?—with an avalanche
of references to whales and an acknowledgement to the poor
worm of a sub-sublibrarian who dug them out for Melville.
Thus I would set in motion a landslide of geographical names,
names on the land of America the beautiful, matched by
names of libraries throughout the land. There could be both
meaning and poetry in such a procedure.

Instead, I shall begin with lines by an American poet and
spokesman, who once served as Librarian of Congress. They
open his poem called "American Letter," and for me, they
express better than any other the beauty of our land and
time's passage over it. Long before the astronauts, the poet
was up there, in imagination; and I prefer his lines to NASA's
press releases. Archibald MacLeish wrote:

We dwell
On the half earth, on the open curve of a continent.
Sea is divided from sea by the day-fall. The dawn
Rides the low east with us many hours;
First are the capes, then are the shorelands, now
The blue Appalachians faint at the day rise;
The willows shudder with light on the long Ohio:

Reprinted from *ALA Bulletin,* 59: 643-648, July-August 1965, by
permission of the author and the publisher (American Library
Association).

The Lakes scatter the low sun: the prairies
Slide out of dark: in the eddy of clean air
The smoke goes up from the high plains of Wyoming:
The steep Sierras arise: the struck foam
Flames at the wind's heel on the far Pacific.
Already the noon leans to the eastern cliff:
The elms darken the door and the dust-heavy lilacs.[1]

Our challenge as citizens is to make a society fit to live
on this great land. Our challenge as librarians is to serve this
great society in all its needs, intellectual and emotional,
practical and recreational, and all under the one roof of a
given library. Thus the good librarian is both doer and dream-
er, producer and poet, statistician and storyteller.

Are there such? Yes, there are. Can we provide more of
them? We can. I stand before you as an incorrigible optimist.
My years of library service and teaching have only strengthened my faith in our mission. I shall speak of some of the good
librarians I have known and know and of ways I believe we
must follow if we are to increase their number. I share Sol
Malkin's concern that in our zeal to give America libraries to
match her greatness, we lose our identity as librarians. Able
librarians should be bookmen first and last, Malkin wrote,
and leave all other noble tasks to sociologists, therapists, and
literacy teachers.

It is thirteen years since I last spoke to a general session
of the ALA. Times have changed more than I have. I'm still
trudging along with the slogan David Clift asked me to speak
to back at the Waldorf in '52. Remember? It's old-fashioned
now. "Books are basic." Our president changed it in *his* opening remarks to "bucks are basic." Both are.

Not having spoken to a general session in all these years
does not mean that I have not spoken. They have been the
speakingest years of my life, the best years of my life. Collecting books and people, building libraries and service, teaching, talking, traveling; around the world, to Asia and Europe,

[1] From "American Letter," by Archibald MacLeish (copyright 1950),
with the permission of the publishers, Houghton Mifflin Co., Boston.

and throughout this great land of libraries, in most of the
states, in such exotic states as Hawaii, Montana, New Mexico,
Texas, Minnesota, Ohio, the Carolinas, New Hampshire (as a
Californian I'm cautious about entering Florida); in and out
of all kinds of libraries and with all kinds of people, not as an
officer or spokesman for any organization, but simply as a
working librarian who has identified himself with books and
writing and the ways they serve people; and whose utterances, simple though they have been, have evoked a thousand
amens.

Now I heed President Castagna's call. Talk about the
state of the union, he commanded; and I believe he meant
not the union of the states, nor that of a man with a maid,
but rather the union of men and women with books—librarianship— and also of books as the fruit of that union between
a writer and his experience. Talk of libraries and readers, he
said, of writers and books, as you have lived with them in this
one world that is our world, the librarian's world that knows
no barriers, no frontiers, temporal or terrestrial.

Nowadays it is fashionable for speakers, especially
librarians, to avoid the personal, to embrace the plural, to
generalize and become unrecognizable as individuals. In asking me to speak, however, I know that our president didn't
want me to give a committee report. I won't.

Nor will I echo his eloquent inventory of our national
library needs. What they need is meeting, not meetings; they
need satisfying, not speechifying. We have many groups who
deserve better library service. My interest, however, is in the
individual whose multiplication makes the group, in the single
person who reads one book at a time and reads that book,
not for what it is, but for what it says and does to him, who
reads books for their alchemical power, their power to turn
clay into gold, to transform something common into something precious.

If each and every one of you has not been changed at
least once by the impact of the author and his power of
projecting himself into your mind and heart so that you
think and feel and act differently, if this has not happened to

you, not once, but time and again from childhood on, then you have wasted your time; you have been drugged, not alchemized, by books.

It is Emerson I return to time and again for inspiration, consolation, confirmation. He spoke with no voice but his own. "For the essential thing is heat," he said, "and heat comes of sincerity. Speak what you do know and believe; and are personally in it; and are answerable for every word."

I must add one more quotation from Emerson. "I hate quotations," he said. "Tell me what *you* know."

My interest in writing and writers was inevitable, for nothing in librarianship is more basic than writing and writers, the process and the people who produce information. Yes, I recognize the uses of nonbook materials; yet I don't love them. They are like some of your relatives. You recognize them, but you don't love them or want to live with them. Put it down as one of the limitations of my nature. In my beginning was the book and I hope to end with the book. I envy Petrarch's end, death taking him in the act of enchantment— I mean reading. I must confess, however, that I do collect audio-visual materials: Mozart on recordings, library buildings on postcards.

My work as librarian has enabled me to face two ways: back to the human sources of books, forward to the human uses of books. I have been concerned with the act of writing, whether it be creative or scholarly, and with the act of reading, be it by scholars or by children. And I have found libraries to be perfect laboratories in which to observe these two acts, without which there would be no librarians. No us.

Let me digress now and unload some troubles on you. You are all young and gay; you have the week ahead of you; while I am old and gray and have to go home in the morning, back to the classroom for the rest of the summer session.

What's wrong with librarians? I have been asking this question and answering it in different ways throughout my life. No, not throughout. In my boyhood it never occurred to me, for I was a favored reader in the South Pasadena Public Library, whose librarian, dear Nellie Keith, never had "no" in her vocabulary.

It was in high school that things went wrong. Its library was merely a study hall. And college was not much better. In my day, the college library lacked books. It had more rules than books. This was not good. At university in France, it was worse. The library had books, but they were untouchable. The librarian regarded everyone who entered as a potential thief. I guess I didn't have an honest face, then. That old man in skull cap and slippers trailed me from shelf to shelf, and every time I reached for a book, he said "no."

Whatever led me to become a librarian when I had such a poor opinion of those who either said "no" or wanted to know why I wanted a certain book? Once I went to a public library (not in France) and asked if they had the Kama Sutra. "What do you want *that* book for?" the librarian asked. I looked her dead in the eye and said, "So I can learn how better to make love." She disappeared, and after a long wait, a male page brought me the book. I never did see *her* again.

So why did I become a librarian, when what I really wanted to be was a writer? That's easy to answer. Because I had the fate and the fortune to meet the most yea-saying librarian I have ever known, the gayest, toughest, most literate, and persuasive recruiter of all. A woman, of course. Althea Hester Warren, God bless her memory. She was our ALA president twenty years ago.

For me, she personified what's right with librarians. She radiated belief, affection courage, and conviction. She gave off Emerson's heat. She loved beauty; she read books; she knew writers. Miss Warren never failed to identify herself as a librarian and her library with beauty, with books, with writers and readers. She was unafraid of controversy. She had more courage than most men. Although she was not a housekeeper, her house was well kept. Miss Warren seated me beside her desk, pulled out a drawer, and a cloud of recruiting literature enveloped me. A pink cloud.

"It's easy," she said. "All you have to do is go back to school for a year and get a professional degree."

"I don't want to go back to school," I protested. "I'm nearly thirty years old and I have four mouths to feed. And besides I want to be a writer. I don't want to be a librarian."

Miss Warren lit up even brighter. I felt the heat. "You want to be a writer!" she exclaimed. "We *need* writer-librarians. We need another Edmund Lester Pearson. You have read *Murder at Smutty Nose,* haven't you?" (I didn't dare tell her I hadn't. But I have now; and it's just out in paperback. *You've* all read it, of course.) She paused, then resumed the attack. "You belong in an academic library," she said. "There you'll have time to write."

I believed her. I did what she said I must do. And time proved her both right and wrong. I went back to school and became certificated. And finally I got a job in an academic library; and after six years I became head of it (it *was* right after the war and there *was* a personnel shortage); and for seventeen years I hung on to the tail of the young bull of a UCLA library. I ran it; it ran me. We ran together. Did I have time to write? Sure I did. There were always twelve hours of every day left me free by the library. I had time to write and I became a writer, though not universally acclaimed.

If you hold a library job that requires only eight hours of your time, then you have sixteen hours left for your own uses. What you do with them determines who you are and what you become. And what you *don't* do in your free time also determines who you are and what you become. You know *my* list of don'ts: bridge, chess, movies, TV, golf, entertainment, amusement, exercise. Friends. Family. Fanaticism, of course, on a graded scale. Grade yourself.

What's wrong with librarians is not that they are mostly not writers or readers. The world does not lack writers, and I have found librarians to be among the best of all readers.

No, it is that librarians don't spend enough time—working time and free time—identifying themselves and their libraries with writers and readers; don't make it their business, always, to encourage living writers by collecting and displaying their books and manuscripts; and by speaking and writing, to their fellow librarians and in their communities, about writing and reading. I don't mean just belles lettres. No. Everything under the sun. As wide as Dewey; as deep as LC. All knowledge is our province. We are the truest of universalists, if not unitarians.

Althea Warren exemplified for me the perfect librarian.
In 1937, when I first worked in the Los Angeles Public
Library before an opening occurred at UCLA, she encouraged
me to exhibit the books and manuscripts of John Steinbeck
and, even more daring, the manuscripts and books of D. H.
Lawrence. Not only that. She asked Aldous Huxley to speak
on Lawrence in the library's lecture room. That was pretty
far out for Los Angeles in 1937.

When Miss Warren agreed to let me arrange an exhibit of
Lawrence, I thought I would test her. I had just come from
library school, where Sydney Mitchell had taught us to be
free spirits. So I asked Miss Warren, "May I include *Lady
Chatterley's Lover?*" Her smile was a wee bit wicked. "Use
your judgment," was her reply. "The library has only one
copy and you might create a demand we couldn't satisfy." I
left it out. No one ever got ahead of Althea Warren, least of
all Larry Powell.

I don't believe librarians should come together, ever,
even when their gatherings are of themselves alone, without
the recognition of books, their writers and readers. This
should be our primary holy service. Afterward, if there is
time, we can make room for housekeeping, for mechanics,
for all those necessary secondaries.

What's wrong with librarians today is that we behave as
housekeepers when we appear in public, and then we are hurt
when the public takes us for such.

Recently I saw a copy of the proceedings of a workshop
on public libraries. It ran for several days and involved some
leading public librarians. The proceedings fill more than a
hundred pages. In those pages there is no mention by anyone
of a specific book or of those transcendent acts of writing
and reading which are the blood and the bone and the mar-
row of librarianship.

Am I saying that it should have been a workshop on
writing and reading? No. Although that wouldn't be a bad
thing for librarians to do. I *am* saying that it is shocking that
librarians could speak for three days and a hundred pages
without someone, somehow, perhaps unconsciously, once

referring to books, to a book, to any book. It's like a work-shop of clergymen who never refer to God.

Wherever I go on my travels, I carry touchstones which I apply to librarians. Bibliographical touchstones in the form of simple questions: Who are your local writers? Has your library collected their manuscripts as well as their books? Which were the first books printed in your city? Does your library have them?

Or geographical touchstones: What mountain is it that I saw as our plane was landing? Have you climbed it? Are there books about it? I flew into El Paso once, westbound from Houston, and the first question I asked Helen Farrington, when I reached the new public library with its mural by Tom Lea, was what was that great peak to the north as we approached El Paso?

"Must have been Guadalupe," she replied. "It's the highest point in Texas."

Carl Hertzog, the Southwest's finest printer, was there in her office with us, and he got into the act, pulling a copy of *Coronado's Children* off the shelf, turning to a passage and reading aloud to us lines in which J. Frank Dobie paid tribute to those librarians,

Who preside over the genial branches of the Grasshoppers' Library in the sunshine of the Pecos, beside the elms and oaks on Waller Creek, down the mesquite flats on the Nueces River, up the canyons of the Rio Grande, under the blue haze of the Guadalupes, deep in the soft Wichitas, over the hills of the San Saba, and in many another happily remembered place, where I have pursued "scholarly enquiries" I cannot name.

O bless his memory, that great good Texan-American, J. Frank Dobie, writer and reader and friend of libraries!

The good librarian knows the answers, as Helen Farrington did. This kind of local omniscience is not in style today, when our interests are drawn to outer space; and yet I have had many memorable encounters with librarians who were encyclopedists on what was nearest to them.

When that Oklahoman turned Californian Bill Holman

was a Texan, I visited him once in San Antonio, and I came
away remembering not only the Alamo, but the Mission San
José, the San Antonio River, Our Lady of the Lake, and
Sister Jane Marie and the saintly Mother Superior to whom
she introduced me; and the ride I had on the marble elephant
that lures children to the Public Library's Harry Hertzberg
Circus Collection and its joyous curator, Leonard Farley,
himself a one-time circus performer. As I boarded the plane,
Holman pressed on me a guidebook, just to make sure of my
facts when henceforth I spoke as a Texan.

In Minneapolis—St. Paul I told my host, Jim Holly, the
Macalester College librarian, that I wanted to follow the
Mississippi as far as possible enroute to Rochester, where the
Minnesota Library Association was meeting. I wanted to see
the confluence of the St. Croix and the Mississippi, don't ask
me why. Holly knew the way; he knew what to see and to
say on the way; he knew the literature of the upper Mississippi; and, in short, he filled me with pride to be in the company
of a librarian who was an unassuming local authority.

And that night, during my talk at the conference, when
I expressed the further desire to see where the Mississippi
rises in Lake Itasca, I was flooded by offers of northern librarians and trustees to take me there, the very next morning,
as soon as day broke. Great land of rivers and lakes *and*
librarians!

When Ed Castagna left the Southwest for Maryland, I
first lamented our loss, then came to rejoice in the way he
swiftly studied and absorbed the local facts of history, geog-
raphy, and folklore there on the eastern sea frontier. Give us
more such cultural transplants!

In our past and in our present there are indeed librarians
to revere and to emulate. Our president and our president-
elect and I, all three of us, were fortunate to have studied
under Dean Sydney Mitchell, that tough Canadian Californian who never softened up; and here tonight are those who
hail Louis Round Wilson as their saint of library service.

There is something wrong with any librarian who fails to
identify with one or more of his predecessors, finding in them

strength for weakness, faith for doubt, joy for despair, going back and pressing forward along the great lifeline of library service which links us all together in our profession.

The library school year should be the crucial year, when we are marked for life by the imprint of a teacher or two. No one who studied at Columbia with Miriam Tompkins was ever the same again. Likewise Frances Clarke Sayers, whose lifetime of library service and teaching in many parts of the country ended last week with her retirement, transfused all around her with her own joyous vitality and discriminating taste. Her newly published volume, *Summoned by Books,* will carry these qualities on and on, beyond our time, to a writer's best immortality. She will never be lost to us, as long as books are read.

No subject taught in library school need be dull. Maurice Tauber and Seymour Lubetzky bring to technical services a world of life and light. To hear Robert Hayes on data processing is a revelation and to watch him illuminate a blackboard is to see an artist in the great tradition of mathematical truth that goes clear back to Euclid.

If I am remembered as a library school dean, it might be because I brought Frances Sayers and Robert Hayes together. It was they who planned a conference on the effect of computers upon children. 1984 is nearer than we think.

It follows then that great teachers deserve the best students. What we need is fewer and better librarians. It is crazy to talk of 20,000 or 30,000 or 50,000 vacancies in library work. We never can and never should try to train professional librarians on such a scale.

We must redefine library education and the standards for library schools. I do not believe in mass recruiting. Too many culls have to be eliminated. Or aren't. Then you in the field get them and blame us in the schools. We should sharp shoot, not scatter shot, to bring down our pigeons. We are in competition with other professions. Our recruiting literature should not be obviously such. Jesse Shera ought to be relieved of administration and teaching and paid to work full time as a writer. And the same goes for Neal Harlow. They are two of our best writers. Don't think I am trying to shut down Rutgers and Western Reserve!

We need a rich fellowship program to bring top college graduates into library schools. How to finance it? Foundations? No. How then? Ourselves. Embrace tithing. Give a tenth of all we earn to perpetuate and improve our profession. We should spend as much, each of us, on library education as we spend on entertainment, tobacco, alcohol, travel.

I suggest to library conference exhibitors that they give to fellowships the same amount they spend on parties and dinners for those who attend conferences. Lord, what riches!

And we should reward recruiters. Offer a bounty, payable to the recruiter, one half upon enrollment of the recruit, the other half upon graduation.

> We dwell
> On the half earth, on the open curve of a continent.
> Sea is divided from sea by the day fall.

MacLeish gave us the land in these words of his poem, and on this land, in the past hundred years, we have built great libraries. It is truly a great land of libraries. And this greatness is not necessarily of size, but of degree.

For there are great little libraries throughout this land of libraries, whose greatness lies simply in their having the right book at the right time for the right reader. Such a one I found to be the public library of Nogales, Arizona, down on the border of Mexico, neighboring the state of Sonora.

I had been elsewhere in Arizona, and the book I wanted was out in use when I asked for it in a large library. Who can object to the use of books? Yet I was trying to finish a book of my own, writing to a deadline, and I desperately needed Bolton's edition of the Anza Expedition, the first overland trek of Spanish colonists from Arizona into California led by Captain Juan Bautista de Anza in 1778, a short, heroic journey of a thousand men, women, children, and livestock, across the desert and over the mountains into the promised land, a journey repeated since then a thousand times over by millions of people, migrating from east to west and now into orbit to God knows where.

So in passing through Nogales (the name means wild walnut in Spanish), and before crossing into Sonora, where I was to buy a big clay pig-bank, I stopped at the new public library, beautifully made of adobe bricks and mesquite timbers, went to the desk and asked my $64 question: "Do you have the Bolton Anza set?"

Without saying a word, the librarian led me to a case in the reading room, opened it, and said proudly, "Our Arizona collection is small but choice. And it is for building use only, if you don't mind."

"Bless you," I said. "You deserve the Lippincott award."

For the Anza set was there, *it was there,* all five volumes, and I fell on it the way Anza's people fell on the promised land.

Isn't this the heart of the matter, the very essence of library service? That we have what is needed, for him who needs it, in the time of his need. And to know what we have, who we are, and how to do what we must do for those who need us, be they poor or rich or neither, and in this knowledge to be proud, a pride derived from service to others. Then and only then will we deserve the word "professional." It is all profoundly simple. Let us not complicate it.

This great land of libraries deserves a great band of librarians. And by great I do not mean the greatness of numbers, but rather the greatness of knowledge, of skill, and of dedication. This is our challenge. I share your faith that we will meet it. □

THE LIBRARY:
THE GREAT POTENTIAL IN OUR SOCIETY?

Verner W. Clapp

We are assembled under a banner that reads, "The Library—
The Great Potential in our Society." If this device means
what it seems to mean it says *the* great potential, not merely
a great potential.

Let me ask you what other groups could, without
tongue in cheek, meet under a similar motto? Could farmers?
Or manufacturers? Or merchants? Or engineers? Or diplo-
mats? Or educators? Or poets? Or philosophers? Or
theologians?

The answer to this question must of course depend on
one's view of the universe and of man's place in it, but I suspect that most of us here might find it a little amusing, and
requiring some explanation, if we should find farmers or
manufacturers or merchants or engineers or lawyers claiming
their fields of endeavor as *the* great potential of our society—
even while we would be quite willing to grant the great and
even necessary contributions which the activities of these
groups make. When we get to medicine we might have
qualms; we might sympathize with the point of view (especially if we felt an attack of influenza coming on) but
might upon reflection be inclined to dispute the claim out of
unwillingness to grant that the health of the whole derives

from the sum of the mere physical health of the parts, important as that may be to each of us as individuals. But when we come to the educators, philosophers and theologians we would really have trouble, for these have long staked out large claims in that very Klondike in which we have planted our flag—a territory which I shall call, for want of a better term, man's participation in and enjoyment of the universe.

But we are all librarians and friends of libraries here today, and we can be pardoned if we ignore these other claims. I can safely maintain our thesis, assured that I am preaching to the already converted.

Would it shock you then if, instead, I should deny our motto, and maintain that there are greater potentials for the benefit of society than those which library work possesses; that libraries are but the creatures and the housekeepers of more dominant, dynamic, contributive and ultimate activities —of education, the law, the making of consumer goods, of religion, of historical curiosity, of the arts, and even of farming? Would it shock you if I reminded you that no librarian has ever won the Nobel prize; that libraries do not produce; that they are merely tools among other tools for the purposes of those who support them—tools to be resharpened to these purposes through the silent power of the purse if they appear to cut aslant the lines prescribed, and to be thrown away if they continue perversely askew? Would it shock you if I reminded you that in several of the largest countries of the world libraries are deliberate instruments of indoctrination, and that in our own country librarians have been found to trim their book selection in defiance of their professional judgements from fear of attack by forces of unreason and obscurantism? Would it shock you if I reminded you that out of just such fears our country has rearranged what many of us thought to be one of our best showcases abroad of our way of life—the information libraries—restricting them instead to instruments of immediate foreign policy? Or that not very long ago American public libraries were being asked to become propaganda agencies for a particular view of life?

I remember an address given by Jonathan Daniels, the

editor of the *Raleigh News and Observer,* before a group of librarians about 1940. What's this tosh about libraries and freedom, he essentially asked, pointing out that in a country notable for its education, its scholarship, its science, *and* its libraries, Nazism had taken over completely in one decade and brought the whole world to war in less than another. How can one speak of libraries as citadels of freedom when they can equally well serve as opium dens of enchanted idleness or—even worse—as agencies for perversion and distortion of the truth, and as mechanisms for enforcing the big lie?

But let's not be bitter about it; take it easy. Let's drive out into the country, find the nearest town and see what happens. Let's stop here for the night. Reading matter? Yes; here are examples of the popular periodical press, with an article or two that should genuinely inform and some stories that might genuinely amuse. Also examples of the baser sort, mere trash and waste of time and spirit. Is there a public library in this town? After numerous inquiries we find someone who knows where the public library is, and we visit it. Dingy, dreary, dogeared and dead! Stupid people and stupid books that no one reads, that no one should read! Is this the great potential of our society? Heaven forbid! Let's go back and watch the moon's reflection in the river until it's time to go to bed.

What do we say to these things, we who meet under the emblem "Libraries—The Great Potential in our Society"?

I say these things are true, perhaps regrettably true, though I am not altogether sure of that. But I also say that, despite these things, libraries are *the* great *potential* in our society—and in this phrase I emphasize both words, "the" and "potential."

In human affairs nothing has use but is also subject to abuse. To tell us that libraries have been abused is not news. What has not? Food, drink, power, pleasure? To tell us that libraries have failed of their highest achievement because of neglect or ignorance or fear or favor, that they have served to excuse idleness and irresponsibility, that they have been debauched and perverted to assist desperate schemes and inhumane ends—all this is but the reverse of a coin, of which the obverse proclaims, in our motto of today, that the capacity for abuse is but a measure of potentiality of use.

Let me ask you to consider with me, what does society (to put it no higher than that) ask of one of its members, and what would it promise him in return.

I would say, in answer to this question, that principal among the things that society requests of and would grant to its members are the following:

That he govern himself
That he love truth and hate falsehood
That he benefit from the experience of others
That he be informed
That he be accurate
That he have perspective
That he be generous, forgiving, and humane
That he be intellectually and emotionally tolerant
That he have reverence, wonder, and awe
That he know, cherish and defend the freedom of the mind
That he pull his weight in the work of the world
That he see and understand himself as a member of his immediate group and execute the responsibilities that this association demands
That he see and understand himself as a member of still larger communities—his city, his country, society as a whole, the world of nature, and eventually the universe—and execute the responsibilities which these memberships, too, demand
That he have interests wider than mere bed and board
That he cultivate his imagination
That he perceive beauty and seek and relish it
That he give back to society at least in measure proportionate to what he received, and that—hopefully, he leave the world a better place for having served a term in it
That he get the sense of accomplishment, that he get enjoyment—even excitement—out of his stay on earth.

As I read this list I am impressed by several things. The first is the enormity of the task which society demands, and justly demands, of each and every one of us—a task which, if we really bent to it, could profitably occupy every minute of many days for each one that is normally allotted. Again I am impressed, as men have been impressed in every age, by how much there is to know, how much to do, how much to enjoy; and meanwhile time, too little time, is all we have. But secondly, I am impressed by the fact that for many of the items on the list the library offers a principal road to achievement, and for almost every item one of the fastest and furtherest roads, once one's feet have been placed in it through other experiences.

I do not mean, of course, that the reading of *Lorna Doone* can substitute for falling in love, or that the writing of a term paper on the Peloponnesian War will produce a regard for accuracy quite as effectively as being docked a day's pay for the careless use of an adding machine. The beauty of the mountains and the sea existed for us before we saw Mt . Fumi through Hokusai's curling wave, and we wondered at the stars before we read about red dwarfs or white giants or the great nebula in Andromeda. As children we played like practiced politicians upon our parents' complex emotions of affection and pride, vexation and vanity long before Machiavelli showed us how these arts could be cynically employed in affairs of state, or before we learned that the science of management consists essentially in a rationalization of what we practiced as children from innocent and instinctive response to environment.

All this is to say that education does not, for the greater part, begin in the library, though it often does so, and should always continue there. But it is also to say this. Formal education can only command, in terms of minutes and hours, a small proportion of the entire life span. And the other educative experiences of life tend to become repetitious and to lose their educative effect, unless enriched, extended, rationalized and given perspective, challenged and matured by comparison with the experiences of others. Where else but in

the library can this experience be found already sifted, recorded, and organized? Where else can it be consulted so
quickly, surely, amply and effectively?

It is trite to say that libraries constitute the communal
memory of mankind—the repository in which its experience,
as far as it has been recorded, may be consulted and applied.
But let me remind you how short a time, in racial terms, this
memory has existed. How many eons did it take before mankind could develop a language and find the sounds with
which to express ideas? How many eons more to discover
that these grunts and clicks, these vocables, could be expressed in graphic form? All but the very slightest traces of
man's experience during those countless ages of painfully
won knowledge—the years in which fire and clothing, agricul-
ture, the identification of useful plants, domestication of
wild animals, the wheel, family life, communal government,
legal systems were all invented—all this is lost to us. Our certain knowledge of that experience commences at only approximately the time at which man began to assemble libraries—barely three thousand years ago. But the general education, which makes possible the universal use of libraries,
and the recognition of the importance of that use to Every-
man and not just to an intellectual elite—that is scarcely a
century old. If we say that libraries are the great *potential* of
our society, that is because we have hardly as yet even begun
to realize from libraries the services to human welfare and
human enjoyment of which they are capable. The priests of
the moon god Nannar in their temple atop a ziggurat in
ancient Sumeria more than 3,000 years ago knew that they
held in their library the great potential of society; for recorded on their cuneiform tablets was the lore which made it possible for them to predict eclipses and to warn of floods and to
communicate past the barriers of time and space; to bring the
wisdom of ancient councils to the decision of modern dis-
putes, and generally to assist in the stabilization of society
and the welfare of the state. But *we* know that our libraries
are *the* great potential of society—a potential hardly as yet
exploited, holding the certainty of profound effects in the
development of the capacities and the contribution and the
enjoyment of every member of the race.   □

THE TROUBLE WITH LIBRARIES

Louis Shores

Four decades ago, a young man narrowed his choices for a life work to four possibilities. Medicine appealed to him because of the opportunity to relieve suffering. Law promised a gateway to statesmanship and world peace. Education seemed foundational for everything, including the other two. Without apology, he chose librarianship. Forty years later his decision would be the same. He believes now, as he has written and spoken many times: ours is a profession of destiny.

He came to this conclusion even before he had read novelist Jan Struthers' words in *A Pocketful of Pebbles:*

> "... librarianship is one of the few callings in the world for which it is still possible to feel unqualified admiration and respect. Almost every other profession has been more or less debunked, either by skeptical theorists or by the merciless cold daylight of human events."[1]

The years since have confirmed his decision.

As he looks at the noisy and frustrated world which he will, before long, leave, he sees relief in the quiet of libraries. On the brink of nuclear "fail-safe," the generic book holds a foil against disaster. Confronted by a psychosis threat to mankind that dwarfs all previous plagues, there is within the embryo of bibliotherapy a way to mental health. Terrified by

Reprinted from *Tennessee Librarian,* 19: 119-129, Summer 1967, by permission of the author and the publisher (Tennessee Library Association).

the mounting disorders of demonstration and delinquency, residents of our large cities, and increasingly of our smaller ones, no longer risk after-dark visits without concern for personal safety. Despite soaring incomes, economic inadequacy besets consumers and producers at every turn. Ours is a world of false prosperity, where war, illness, delinquency and poverty stalk human beings as menacingly as at any time in man's history.

Yet there is one profession in this world that can bring hope to a mentally depressed age, within the profession, for which novelist Struther felt unqualified admiration, is the potential to turn the tide of disorder into power for startlingly fresh break-throughs. Even among such feeble starts as librarianship has made to communicate truth and beauty, there are the seeds of innovation so epic as to add new dimensions to the art and science creations to date. What holds us back is our inadequate image, not only as others see it, but as we look at it ourselves.

Each of us made our decision to practice this profession for variations on a basic attraction: we like books; we like people; we like to bring them together. Some of us came to this choice of a life work by elimination: nothing else attracted us more or was possible. Others of us used the profession as a prelude: to teaching, to law, to business, to marriage. Many of us, if not most, however, deliberately decided there was something beyond what most careers offered in this catalysis of books and people; indeed a few had visions of something approaching Revelation.

With such great expectations why is it, then, that at this late date we are still unhappy with our image? Dr. Alice Bryan gave us some clues several years back in her study of the Librarian, as a part of the *Public Library Inquiry*[2], when she summarized

> "Personality inventories filled out by the Inquiry sample of librarians show their median scores to be somewhat below established norms for persons with comparable general education with regard to leadership and self-confidence, but with other measured qualities near the general norms."

Commenting on the nature of our occupation, she observed:

> The work is largely sedentary, performed in a quiet,
> friendly atmosphere, relatively free from the pressures
> and sharp, personal rivalries for place and power that
> characterize much of commercial enterprise. Librarian-
> ship is an occupation with modest pecuniary rewards,
> but with the satisfactions which accompany the render-
> ing of useful public service. It has traditionally been a
> calling within which women were welcomed and could
> rise to the top. It is still carried on preponderantly by
> women.[3]

Whether because of this feminine predominance in our
profession, or for other reasons, Dr. Bryan was able to "con-
struct a personality profile of the 'typical' librarian" that revealed he (or she) "is rather submissive in social situations
and less likely to show qualities of leadership . . . he tends to
lack confidence in himself and to feel somewhat inferior."[4]
According to Dr. Bryan there is no difference in these characteristics between male and female librarians. The only sex
difference, according to the Gamin factor tested by Dr.
Bryan, is that women librarians seem to be somewhat more
feminine than men librarians are masculine.

We may not like these findings. We can contend that the
Public Library Inquiry is now outdated since it was undertaken over a decade ago. Or those of us not now in public librarianship may comfort ourselves that this description does
not apply to academic, school, or special librarians. But the
fact remains that most of us apologize for our image, and
strive valiantly in our recruitment to combat the stereotype
that literature, the movies and television portray when we are
infrequently represented in these media.

If we are honest with ourselves, we must admit both
sides. Our progress in advancing libraries, certainly in recent
years, has been good. With mounting federal aid, we have increased accessibility, measurably. Our means of circulating
books to people become steadily more efficient, despite the
periodic satires about the computer that "it costs more and is
slower, but we *are* automated." We save lots of time photo-

copying what we formerly did by hand, and soon we will be transmitting these copies instantaneously by facsimile to the scientist at his laboratory bench so that he will not have to waste his precious time walking as far even as his decentralized departmental library. The net result may be doubling the present half million scientific reports now published annually. Inevitably this will force *Chem Abstracts* to introduce an index to its index and call for a second White House conference on the information crisis in science.

It is both ways. We have made tremendous strides in gaining financial support for libraries. Mechanical and electronic improvements in circulation have been ingenious. Our edifices have begun to compare in luxury with movie palaces and night clubs, even with high rise office buildings and Miami Beach resort hotels. Furnishings sparkle with the latest gadgets and the brightest colors. Salaries for librarians are not only comparable, but *U.S. News and World Report* in recent months revealed that our profession tied law for first place in beginning pay levels.

But we must also ask ourselves critically, are libraries and librarianship contributing decisively to any of the great issues that confront mankind today? We hover on the brink of a world war that because of science's nuclear triumphs virtually guarantees human extermination. What is our profession doing about that? The World Health Organization reveals that by no means the least threat to our physical well being is the plague of mental illness, which even in the prosperous United States now affects nearly half the population. How concerned has librarianship been with this calamitous threat? Delinquency—adult as well as adolescent—has made sight-seeing in our beautiful national capital city, after dark, hazardous. Differences on our public issues are increasingly communicated not by free discussion and debate, but by disorderly demonstration that is now rarely peaceful. What part have libraries played in that, except occasionally to have its books burned. Against this, it sometimes appears we have been less aroused than against the misinformed citizen groups that remove from the shelves books that become currently great, not to mention profitable, by exhibitioning four-letter words, and blaming their obscenity on the reader, rather than the writer.

Well, we can console ourselves, why pick on librarians? If our statesmen haven't been able to prevent war in all of these centuries, what chance have we? Certainly, what more can we hope to do with knowledge than circulate it through books to more and more people? As for health and delinquency, these are for the doctors and the policemen; obviously they are not in our department. As for today's literary output, although related to our work, who are we to challenge celebrated names among contemporary authors and critics?

Translated into specifics, this is what Dr. Bryan may have meant by her personality profile for the typical librarian. Perhaps we are, as she observes, "rather submissive in social situations and less likely to show qualities of leadership." It may be that we do tend "to lack confidence" and "to feel somewhat inferior." Have we the courage to look at ourselves as they do who have given our image the stereotype? Each of us, of course, will touch up our professional portrait differently. What I am about to say represents only one librarian's opinion, after four decades or more in the profession.

The trouble with librarians, in my opinion, is fundamentally what Dr. Bryan's profile of the librarian exposed. Some of you know the thesis I have now repeated several times in my writings and speakings. We suffer from what I call an ancillary complex. Part of this complex, I concede, comes from the nature of our profession. Libraries are some of the few places in our staccato existence where the legato mood can still be found. Lately we have been parodied in good musical drama like the *Music Man* (and this may alert you on the unsophisticated literary standard I shall advocate later). You will recall Marian the Librarian, who nevertheless does get her sales *Man*, enforcing library quiet with "s-s-h-h—punctuated" song and dance in the book stacks. Less acceptable is my favorite columnist Henry McLemore's contention that library quiet has been over-enforced. I want our traditional climate to be maintained for the good of mankind. I believe our tendency toward the discotheque must be balanced with some time in the bibliotheque. The only hope I see for our national jitters is to compensate for the current attraction to "where the action is" with some time for meditation and introspection in our churches and libraries.

Because of this traditional and desirable library quiet, I am sure we have developed an occupational diffidence. I can illustrate it with my own World War II experience. Probably no profession prepares a soldier less for military service than librarianship. After tiptoeing and whispering for a lifetime of library work I found myself suddenly in the marching, noisy tempo of an army base. When something called V.O.C., through voluntary waiving of IIIA draft status for enlistment earned me the right to enter officer training, I understood at once the librarian's handicap. Part of it was, of course, the stories I was used to hearing and telling at professional meetings, would fall flat on their face with G.I.'s. (After the War, the reverse happened also, and more embarrasingly, especially when I found myself subconsciously starting an illustration with an army tale that didn't quiet belong in mixed company.) But the main part came in something called "Command." To overcome my librarian habit of pussy-footing, I practiced up and down the beach of Miami with a similarly handicapped librarian

Squads Right!

Imagine the further contrast when I found myself later (1942) in my overseas theatre of war, designated C.B.I., and these initials stood not for Cumulative Book Index but for China-Burma-India!

Readily, I admit our occupational climate is not conducive to the opposite personality traits of those Dr. Bryan found in us. No wonder her typical profile of the librarian showed submissive characteristics and tendencies to lack self-confidence and suffer from an inferiority complex. Perhaps this explains the ancillary complex of our profession, the inclination to underestimate our place in society and compensate for this by reasserting ever more zealously our support of other things and people.

Do not misunderstand my contention, please. I believe in most of what we are doing. We should continue to serve as conscientiously as we have in the past, teachers and professors in our schools and colleges, as well as their students; citizens in our communities in all occupations and walks of life; specialists in industry, government, and other agencies that represent the clientele of special librarianship. But I believe, in addition to our ancillary functions, that we also have initiatory ones that deserve a different kind of support from those we serve, an ancillary support from them to our effort.

Let me begin with the first of four specifics. I consider our profession based on a discipline as substantive as any found in our university curricula, for academic as well as for professional education. If we accept the dictionary definition, discipline represents

"The studies collectively embraced in a course of learning, a branch of instruction, a science or art, or the training resulting from a course of such studies."[5]

then, of course, we have a discipline, whether we call it Library Science or Library Art, as I have suggested,[6] or just Bibliography as defined by Dean Raymond Irwin of the University of London School of Librarianship. Yet there are many librarians who insist we are ancillary, only, with no content of our own, and at best, supportive to the predatory subjects in our curriculu

One has only to live on a university campus as long as I have to realize the hierarchy of disciplines. Some subjects are, of course, more blue blood than others. Time was when theology, Latin, Greek, philosophy and history were the respectable ones, and the sciences young upstarts. Indeed, we are all aware historically of the medieval universities' quadrivium and trivium. But campus fashions have changed. The physical sciences rule the roost, followed by Bi Sci. History retains its former respectability by resisting identification with the social sciences, which range in substance, according to some, from political science and economics down to sociology. Education is still on the other side of the curriculum railroad track. As for the Humanities, Science has reluctantly conceded there might be another culture, and out of respect for age permit philosophy, language and literature to co-exist in the community of scholars.

What about the library. No question. Like motherhood no one opposes them. The Library is, some times, even referred to as the heart of a college, or school. But we all know from experience, when times get hard the administrator may all but amputate this heart. What about the librarians? They are highly regarded by faculty generally, as long as they remain in their place, as second class citizens in the academic community. Librarians exist to retrieve materials, much like Fido bringing his master the daily newspaper. At best, they can search out a fact or compile a list of sources for the classroom teacher or researcher to evaluate and interpret. This is so because the librarian has no substantive discipline of his own, according to professors of the acknowledged subject matter.

To some extent this is confirmed by many of us in the profession of librarianship. While on the one hand contending for faculty status, (the very fact of having to contend for it documenting our inferior standing) some of us insist ours is an ancillary service to the substantive, so-called, disciplines. There are others among us, who agree with administrators, since we do not teach in classrooms, that we should not have faculty status. How these administrators and librarians will square this with the inevitable trend to independent study, and revolt against the lockstep of the classroom remains to be seen.

Fortunately there are many among us who believe that our profession is based on a discipline of deep content. A few suggest that our discipline may be the sum total of all the rest, and therefore prerequisite. To begin with, our present library school curriculum, despite its imperfections, which are no more than other curricula, (if we can judge by the series of recent critiques of all levels of U.S. education, from preschool to graduate school, embracing such specialties as medicine, law, engineering and pedagogy) I consider as

contentual as the most substantive of our university subjects,
not only at Florida State, but in universities elsewhere both
in the United States and abroad. These exchanges involve
doctoral committee membership since 1943; mutual class
visits followed by comparative discussions for teacher improvement; joint classes; our unique 500 course on literature
searching for graduate students in all other departments on
the campus[8]; and finally extra-library school visiting lecturers
and master's committee members' contributions to library
education.

From a background of 38 years of college and secondary
school classroom teaching I submit that from my first-hand
knowledge the course area we call variously "Library Foundations," "Library and Society," or "Principles of Librarianship" has a content comparable in scope and depth to most
of the social sciences I have studied, observed or taught. Our
unit on professional ethics, usually included in this area, has
earned the respect of at least one philosophy professor who
participated. The library history part has recently interested
historians so much as to enlist them in our common enterprise, the quarterly *Journal of Library History*, published
continuously since January 1966.

A second library school course area of comparability is
library classification. Theoretically it is related to that branch
of philosophy known as epistemology; what do we know?
Our creators of library systems in modern times, from Dewey
to Ranganathan have given us models of knowledge organization as significant as those of Mendeleyev for chemistry, or
Linnaeus for biology. Although this is the era of reclassifica-
tion to L.C., and the debunking of D.C., some striking paral-
lels can be drawn between the work of Melvil Dewey in library classification, and the classifications of his counterparts
in chemistry and biology. In some ways, Dewey's dimension
of mnemonics can be compared with Mendeleyev's first use
of valence as a basis for ordering the elements. Similarly,
comparisons can be drawn between the classes, divisions, sections concept of D.C., and the classification principles applied
by Linnaeus to clarifying the relationships within the

kingdom of botany, zoology and mineralogy, and employing generic and specific names. The more I read about the Russian chemist, and the Swedish naturalist, the higher I hold my head about the U.S. librarian.

A third library school course area embraces all of the book selection offerings, and since 1947, the evaluation and selection of other formats of the generic book, some times called audio-visual materials, or educational media. Not so long ago, a very sophisticated young woman with bachelor's from an elite eastern woman's college, who had majored in English literature, and earned a master's from Harvard with accent on Browning, entered Florida State Library School. She was also on leave from an ivy league college library, where her intellectual colleagues had convinced her library school was a necessary hurdle to the union card, if she were to earn a genteel living before the right man came along. Expecting a *Library Journal*-like letter to the editor denouncing library school as the only failure in an otherwise perfect U.S. educational system, from grammar through graduate school, imagine my surprise when she began unequivocally in a requested conference, "I am an English major of two pretty fair institutions of higher education. The most stimulating course in literature I have ever had has just been completed here in this library school—Miss Gregory's course in Children's Literature."

My response, as I recall it, was rather mediocre satire. 'You can't say that. There is no substance to the discipline of librarianship. Everybody knows that; even librarians. If you doubt it read the letters to the editor by last year's graduates."

I was immediately sorry, I remember, and apologized. Satire is my unfavorite form in anything from conversation to literature. Most of all, I try to avoid it with students. It was inadequate acknowledgment for confirmation of what I believe earnestly: our book courses are as solid as any. The same can be said for our courses in basic book selection, in adult and young people's literature.

For years I have known that the kind of basic reference course Fannie Cheney and I teach includes a literature form as rich in examples as almost any other—essays, oratory, letters, satire, humor, and perhaps even poetry, drama and fiction. Consider such classics as the *Annual Register,* founded over two centuries ago by Edmund Burke; or the century-old yearly *Statesman's Yearbook,* whose first hundred years of history was so absorbingly chronciled by the present London editor, Dr. Samuel Steinberg in his recent article for the *Journal of Library History.*[10] Read the prefaces to such reference classics as the *Thesaurus* of the London physician of a century ago, Peter Mark Roget; *Dictionary of National Biography,* by Leslie Stephen; *A Dictionary of Slang and Colloquial English,* by Eric Partridge; to *Bartlett's Familiar Quotations,* heralded by Oliver Wendell Holmes over a hundred years ago, and especially the forewords to the 10th edition by Nathan Haskell Dole, and to the 11th edition by Christopher Morley, both editors of this indispensable perennial; and ponder all over again the question what makes literature great.

Which brings me to my second specific. If we unjustifiably underestimate our discipline, we are even more diffident in matching our professional evaluations of books with appraisals by the sophisticated literary critics. Some years back a librarian discovered that the ratio of Faulkner titles in the *Fiction Catalog* to those of novelist Bess Streeter Aldrich was as two to nine. There was much scurrying to adjust in the next edition.

Not one among us had the affrontery to stand by our earlier selection. What could *Lantern in Her Hand,* for example, offer in comparison with *The Sound and the Fury* or *Sanctuary.* Why should a relatively unknown novelist be favored over a Nobel winner, and Pulitzer, later, too.

I know that the critics generally consider Faulkner "unmatched by any other American novelist in narrative intensity, descriptive vividness, and range of characterization."[11] I hope you will forgive me, but at my age I must be honest about my literary limitations, and expose my rather naive art biases. I have tried very hard to appreciate Faulkner, but he continues to remain somewhat obscure for me, given to "rather excessive ornateness and a propensity for the lurid and the horrible." On the other hand, what I know of Bess Streeter Aldrich indicates wholesomeness, at least. The late Helen E. Haines whose *Living With Books* most librarians admire, advocating "an intelligent effort to replace inferior fiction by more excellent work on the same general type" suggested "a novel by Bess Streeter Aldrich should satisfy, on a superior level, even a devotee of Harold Bell Wright."[12]

So I begin my contribution to the literary theme of this convention with dissent, primarily, with contemporary realism in fiction and drama. I disagree with today's dominant school of literary criticism. I object to the current artistic accent on the negative and pessimistic. I do not believe celebration of the ugly will encourage the opposite. In my minority opinion it is less brave to dwell on the sordid, to raise problems, to portray things true to the abnormalities in life, than to seek out the good in man, to offer solutions, to concentrate on the goodness that is found in our daily living.

Let me illustrate. During the last leave in New York to work on the *Encyclopedia* I counted in one series of twenty-three reviews of Broadway plays, opening or internal sentences that read "He has had the courage to expose," and in each case the exposé was a perversion, an addiction, an abnormality of one kind or another. In most of these vehicles the endings were death, frustrations, unhappiness, unsettled problems, self-pity. This was defended as "true to life." Sex dominated usually. I realized that in the modern temper, obscenity was present, I was supposed to have put it there, not the dramatist.

Well, I disagree. There can no longer be any question about librarianship's position on freedom to read or write. Goodness knows, in my six years (one year more than the usual term) as a member of the ALA Intellectual Freedom Committee I defended writers' rights to write as frankly as possible. I participated in communities' public forums about books removed from library shelves. I was in the middle of the *Ruby McCollum* case where the facts finally revealed that, not Florida, but the publisher had banned the sale of that book about an affair between a white doctor and his colored patient. The infamous "bushel basket" case was dropped into my lap, and I contributed to the restoration of those books. But all of those six years something tugged at my conscience.

Were we librarians tending, unintentionally, to promote inferior literature by all this attention to certain titles. Was there a possibility, after all, as Russell Kirk, Bill Couch and other intellectual conservatives contended, that we on the Committee were more vigilant to defend the rights of the dissenters than we were to defend the rights of those who dissented with dissent? Were we balancing our crusade for intellectual freedom with comparable concern for intellectual responsibility?

Let me deal with two current best sellers. Despite exorbitant critical acclaim of Edward Albee's *Who's Afraid of Virginia Woolf,* New York Drama Critics Circle and Tony Awards, *Newsweek's* "brilliantly original—an excoriating theatrical experience," I found the book so incredibly dull that I could not bring myself to attend either the theatre or the movie presentation.

Again, spectacular praise and profit have come to Truman Capote for *In Cold Blood.* My literary standards are apparently out of step with the times. I felt no compassion for the criminals such as some expressed. Nor did I find the writing as good as in, for example, *Breakfast at Tiffany, Other Voices, Other Rooms.* Indeed, I simply had to compel myself to read on in this wordy chronicle, and I accomplished this only by alternate interruptions with reading John G. Fuller's *Incident at Exeter.* Incidentally, speaking of writing, and describing settings, compare, one day, as I did, Capote's job on Holcomb, Kansas, with Fuller's on Exeter, New Hampshire.

I cite these two books only as recent examples of my librarian dissent with the critics, and without apology. Over the years, I believe our professional book selection criteria, when they have not been swayed by the criticism of sophisticated realism, skepticism, negativism, have been nearer to the truth that is beauty. Within our profession, of course, there has been a range of values. I now speak for one librarian only. Because I have read for so many years I have probably developed more than my share of what H. L. Mencken called prejudices. The big four of English 18th Century, and the Big four of Russian 19th century novel writing had an early and persistent influence on my values. So did Tolstoy's *What is Art?* and Upton Sinclair's *Mammonart.* To these I've added some biases of my own.

First, I believe research and realism belong to the sciences, social as well as natural. On this basis I am willing to concede that both Faulkner and Capote do a better job than most of the social scientists who had their day during my Chicago G. S. period. Second, I am now convinced that no great art can be created with reliance on either research or realism. The concern of art is, and should be, in my opinion, with reality, and basically reality is not involved with minute description of physical happenings on this planet, except incidentally, when there are so many worlds and countless eons in infinity. Art owes us a flash of the ultimate, a look into the riddle of the universe such as I am now convinced the scientific method never can give us. Therefore, art must eschew research and return to revelation.

Even such distinguished scientists of this century as Einstein, Whitehead, and Jung have acknowledged in their autobiographical notes that their creative work came out of mysterious flashes totally unrelated to their research. Certainly, such mysterious inspirations have made our great literature that has survived for centuries. For such revelations, I search in the literature of the present, and not in vain. The critics won't like my nominations to the hall of truth and beauty. At Random, I find art in Nevil Shute—*On the Beach,* of course, and *Trustee in the Toolroom.* About the latter one reviewer observed disdainfully, "In it a right guy lives happily ever after at the end." I like James Hilton, probably to the disgust of erudites, when I suggest greatness as well as goodness in *Goodbye Mr. Chips* and *Lost Horizon.* Upton Sinclair's novels from the *Jungle* and *King Coal,* of the earlier days, through *Oil, Boston,* and the more recent Lanny Budd series.

Among Philip Wylie's two dozen fictional works there are near-great ones: *Night unto Night, The Disappearance, Opus 21,* and *Tomorrow.* Hemingway had greatness for me in *The Old Man and the Sea,* and *For Whom the Bell Tolls;* dullness in *Across the River and Into the Trees* and the non-fiction *Death in the Afternoon.* Most of John Steinbeck, much of Priestly, some of Graham Greene have attracted me.

Without cataloging likes further, let me come to the point. Let us stop being ancillary to the literary critic. When we agree with him let's; when we disagree let us have the courage to stand by the choices in our selection aids. Let us recognize we have the intellect, the discrimination, the insight, to develop standards of literary excellence independent of those of the dominant school of literary criticism. Let us become a force, too, and a climate, for the good and beautiful in art. Let us match our vigilance for intellectual freedom with an equal zeal for intellectual responsibility.

My third specific is education. All my professional ife I have heard us declare we must support classroom instruction; we must follow the curriculum; we must, I agree. But we must also help develop that curriculum; overrule if necessary those who have constructed curricula in the past and asked the library to follow the course of study, whether it was good or bad. Above all, we have a role to play in education which may well reverse the sequence of the past. How can we stand aside in the face of the growing independent study movement, when soon there may be little or no classroom instruction to support? Will we be up to doing the actual teaching in carrels? Or will we watch others less oriented perpetuate an instruction against which student revolt is growing?

Specialisms have so distorted the learning of our next generation that students no longer have perspective on this existence. If the researchers who dominate our educational outlook had had their way, in the beginning God would have been a chemist on the first day, a physicist on the second, a botanist on the third, and so forth. Of one thing I am sure, the universe is not organized by our courses of study. And I believe only librarianship, and the discipline of the library art can bring back a *Gestalt* to our education.

My fourth specific is discovery and the frontiers of knowledge. Today research is the only synonym, and this is carried on predominantly by the scientific method. I do not want to be misunderstood. Research and science are here to stay for a long while. Librarianship has done considerable with both in this short period since the activation of the Graduate Library School at Chicago, which first made the profession conscious of the opportunity. But I believe librarianship has the creativity and courage to come up with other approaches for discovering the ultimates in this riddle which represents the universe.

Despite C. P. Snow's contention, we are becoming a one-culture society. Our art, as well as our physical and social environment, have succumbed to the method of science. Yet the fact remains that although science has accomplished much with phenomena, it has been singularly helpless with what Plato called the noumena. Snow's very use of the Second Law of Thermodynamics illustrates not so much the Humanist's neglect of the other culture, as it does the impotence of science when confronted by ultimates. I am less sanguine that the scientific method will ever give us the *why,* even if it does give us the *how* for a number of phenomena like heat-energy relations, absolute zero, the living cell. Perhaps there is a parascience, after all, not dependent upon the senses, that only an unfettered discipline like that upon which our profession is based can conjure with.

My fifth specific is society. There is, for example, a next stage in our drive for world literacy. Even after all of the people can read mechanically there is no assurance they will read critically and intelligently. Witness the low level of some of our commercials, and their apparent popular appeal. We have a job to do, to toughen national minds all over the world to resist subversion in any form, from the west as well as from the east. This is not easy. But we have made significant beginnings with programs like our earlier "Reading With a Purpose," our later American Heritage, and our U.S.I.S. libraries abroad.

The libraries of the world can do very much more.

Every place there is a demonstration instead of a discussion, whether the march is against the favorite target—Washington, L.B.J. and the U.S.A.—or another government as liberal toward protests as ours, that violence must be counted our partial, at least, responsibility. Even if there ever was such a thing as a peaceful demonstration, we will have to admit that ours in the United States are becoming ever more war-like.

I call upon libraries everywhere to revive the old town hall type of meeting. Let the Library Hall become a substitute for the exhibitionism of demonstration. We must help our people document their causes with sources from all sides of public issues. To all of our people we must give the critical faculty to challenge all advocacy. I have never seen a picket sign that could do this. Before I accept even Bertrand Russell's accusations, I want to see his evidence, supported by sources that are not pre-committed.

Perhaps in these five specifics I have telegraphed my faith in our profession. Possibly, I have suggested that we are no more ancillary than any other discipline or profession. I may even have indicated a few areas where others might support us; be the anciallary partner for a change; even admire our deeper substance.

Wrongly or rightly, I believe in our profession. Not with apology, but with conviction that our work has something to offer to mankind beyond anything we have yet included in our role. Call it a mixture of optimism and mysticism. Whatever the ingredients that combine to give us a life work, the faith we profess in librarianship is the stuff of destiny. In my occult sense I know that we are marked to bring mankind closer to the Kingdom. □

REFERENCES
[1] Struther, Jan. *A Pocketful of Pebbles.* Harcourt, 1946.
[2] Bryan, Alice I. *The Public Librarian.* 1952. p. 54.
[3] *Ibid.,* p. 53.
[4] *Ibid.,* p. 39-44.
[5] *Funk & Wagnalls New Standard Dictionary.* 1940. p. 721.
[6] Shores, Louis. "The College of Library Art." *Journal of Library Education.*

[7] Irwin, Raymond.

[8] Clemons, John.

[9] Shores, "We Who Teach Reference."

[10] Steinberg. *Journal of Library History.*

[11] Daniel, Robert W., *Collier's Encyclopedia.* 1960. V. 9, p. 615.

[12] Haines, Helen E. *Living With Books.*

OUR LIBERTIES AND OUR LIBRARIES

Quincy Howe

To talk about our liberties would take as much time as to talk about all our libraries. But there are two liberties that all our libraries promote and it is to these two liberties that I would call attention tonight. The first is freedom to read; the second freedom to choose. The Bill of Rights to our Constitution stresses the more active freedoms of speech and assembly, of press and worship. But there is the right of the hearer to hear, as well as of the speaker to speak; the right of the reader to read, as well as of writer to write. Nor does the matter stop here. A free society gives the hearer the right not to hear; the reader the right not to read: in short, the freedom to choose.

Our libraries promote both the right to read and the right to choose. They promote the right to read because they have made themselves the repositories of the written and printed records of our race. They promote the right to choose when they make these records accessible to the public. "In the beginning was the Word," says the Gospel According to Saint John, but it is through the Book that the Word is recorded and transmitted. And if we call Judaism and Christianity, and Islam, too, religions of the book, surely we may

---

Reprinted by permission from the January 1959 issue of the *Wilson Library Bulletin*. Copyright © 1959 by The H. W. Wilson Company. [Address given at the ALA Liberty and Justice Book Award program at the American Library Association conference in San Francisco, July 1958.]

call our whole culture a culture of the book—not exclusively, of course, but characteristically.

During the Dark Ages, the libraries of Byzantium and of the Greek monasteries preserved the records of Christian and pre-Christian times. The fall of Byzantium coincided with the dawn of the Renaissance and the development of the printing press. From the fifteenth to the nineteenth century, more and more books piled up in more and more libraries from which more and more scholars spread more and more light and learning to more and more people.

The dawn of the industrial era brought still greater changes as the spread of literacy made the library a public, not a private institution. During the nineteenth century our libraries remained repositories of an ever-growing accumulation of knowledge; they still served as laboratories for scholars. But as literacy became universal and as the economies of mass production reduced the cost of books, magazines, pamphlets, and newspapers, a vast, new reading public came into being. The twentieth century library now brings to this public a variety and volume of reading matter that no individual could afford to buy. And in so doing, the modern library serves authors and publishers as well as scholars and the general public.

Consider what would happen if our ten thousand public libraries stopped buying any new books. The experimental novelist, the advance-guard poet, the definitive biographer, the philosopher of history, and the publishers who bring out their works must count on sales to libraries to be able to function at all. You librarians, and others who have to do with the production, distribution, and consumption—if I may use the word—of books know that the book industry is caught in the same cost-price squeeze that grips so many other industries. The publisher cannot double and treble his prices above prewar levels; he must therefore double and treble his sales while increasing his prices perhaps 50 per cent. Book clubs make their selections, judges of book contests make their awards, and all this encourages publishers to take chances they would not otherwise take. All this also spurs authors on to extra effort. But if there were no libraries to bring together all sorts and conditions of readers with all sorts and conditions of books, day in day out, year in year out, our greatest single outlet for the greatest variety of literary talent and scholarly purpose would be largely denied us. I refer, of course, to the bound and printed book.

Since 1900, the bound and printed book, and the libraries which preserve so many old ones and purchase so many new ones, have played an ever-growing role in our national cultural life. For several generations now, nearly all Americans have known how to read and write. By mid-century, however, the steady increase in our high-school and college graduates has multiplied many times over the number of Johnnies and Marys who can read books—a feat that requires something more than mere literacy. The New York *Times* recently noted that of the 525 million books sold in the United States in 1956, 253 million were paperbacks and that 85,000 outlets have between 30 and 50 million copies of such books continuously on display. The low-cost paperback book has thus taken over some of the traffic the libraries alone used to carry. The popular magazines have taken over still more. *Life* claims that more than 28 million people read every one of its fifty-two weekly issues. The *Saturday Evening Post,* which prints more than 3 million copies a week, claims that several times 3 million people spend over three hours on each issue. *Reader's Digest* with a circulation of 10 million copies reaches even more readers but on a monthly, not a weekly basis.

The widening circle of readers who turn to paperback books and popular magazines has not diminished the number of readers who turn to libraries. On the contrary. As the habit of reading becomes more widespread, so does the use of our libraries and the books and periodicals they contain. Nor is this all. The spread of the library habit reflects something more than the spread of the reading habit. The more books people read, the more widely their interests range. But other habits spread more rapidly, and those habits, too, widen the interests of those who acquired them.

MOTION PICTURES

During the first two decades of the present century, the motion-picture habit spread more rapidly than the reading habit had spread in two centuries. At first, motion pictures appealed almost exclusively to illiterates, but as the industry prospered, it widened the narrow horizons of its original, primitive public and at the same time began to open the eyes of the reading public to the birth of a new art form—the greatest, according to H. G. Wells, ever discovered by the human race. The art of black and white photography, now more than a century old, still has much to learn. The newer art of color photography has far more. And the techniques of sound reproduction have made miraculous progress since the first talking picture, thirty years ago. The wonder is not that the art of the motion picture still lags so far behind the arts of the theater, the dance, and music from which it draws so much; the wonder is that the artists, craftsmen, technicians, and scientists who have created the modern motion picture have done so much in so short a time.

The still newer industries of radio and television have learned from the movies—and with the movies—how to make even more rapid technical and aesthetic progress. And radio, like the movies, is now suffering from growing pains, as well as from the competition of television. But nearly all their troubles have to do with economics, not aesthetics; with money, not technique; with management, not performance. And that's because those who create our motion pictures, radio broadcasts, and television performances have learned their skills at two stern and reliable schools—the school of tradition and the school of performance. Management, on the other hand, has had to grapple with problems for which no school, whether of tradition or experience, offers much preparation.

What has all this to do with books and libraries? Not much, to judge from some of those who work in these new fields and pass judgment upon them. For instance, Charles Steinberg, director of press information for CBS Radio has written a new book on public relations, public opinion, and

mass media, entitled *The Mass Communicators* and this is
what he has to say about books, publishers, libraries and the
"book public":

The "book public," unfortunately, is not large when
compared to the public which reads newspapers and/or lis-
tens to radio and watches television. For example, the five
hundred book publishers in the United States issue about
12,500 titles in an average year, including new books and
new editions. Many of these are bought in the relatively few
bookstores around the country or borrowed from the 10,031
public libraries. But the total group reached is, by comparison, a minority one.

But what a minority and what a tribute the author of
The Mass Communicators has paid it. Not only has Dr. Steinberg had to turn to a book to say his say. On the title page,
he proclaims himself Charles Steinberg, Ph.D. Like Dr. Frank
Stanton of the Columbia Broadcasting System, like Dr.
George Gallup of Young and Rubicam, like Dr. Ernest Dich-
ter of the Institute for Motivational Research, Dr. Steinberg
belongs to that growing company of scholars turned admen
(or admen turned scholars) who have blazed the six-lane,
separated toll throughway that now connects the Groves of
Academe with Madison Avenue, USA. These courier-inter-
preters have learned to play rewarding double roles in the
two worlds. On Madison Avenue, their Ph.D. degrees yield
such financial rewards as no mere expert on Chaucer's use of
the semicolon can command on any campus. And in like
manner, when the man in the gray flannel suit wanders
among the academic groves he speaks an occult, compelling
language that combines the meaningless precision of the
social scientist with the glorious nonsense of the advertising
copywriter.

It is not, however, what they say; it is the fact they say
it in book form that imparts authority to these well-groomed
scholars. As Dr. Steinberg's researches have revealed, the
book public is not so large as the radio-television public. But
the book public reads and because the author expresses himself in print he casts a magic spell over those more accustomed

to electronic channels. You know the saying that there is nothing so dead as yesterday's newspaper. But at least its physical body survives its death, and libraries find places on their shelves for yesterday's newspapers, last month's magazines, and last year's books—which sometimes become next year's classics. Libraries also make all this printed matter available, and if the book public which throngs our libraries is a minority so small as to be of no concern to the mass communicators, perhaps that is because book publishers do not try to reach all the book-buying public with every one of the 12,500 titles they turn out—as motion picture, radio and television producers strive always for the greatest possible share of what Gilbert Seldes calls "the Great Audience" in his book of that title. Convinced that few of the mass communicators ever reach all that public at once, Mr. Seldes wrote a book— for how else could he communicate with his fellow beings?— urging that the mass communicators settle for fractions, even small fractions, of the great audience which gets its entertainment and its information from the motion pictures, radio, television, and the popular press.

After Mr. Seldes wrote *The Great Audience,* he wrote *The Public Arts,* which is the name he coined for the kind of entertainment that the mass communicators communicate. More than thirty years ago, his first book, *The Seven Lively Arts,* discussed the popular, or the public, arts of that time and, just recently, CBS produced a television series with that title. Mr. Seldes is one of the sharpest, most outspoken and versatile of our critics. He is the egghead's egghead, the intellectual's intellectual. Yet it is a tribute to the great audience and the public arts of which he writes that his opinions carry weight and that he contributes regularly to the *Saturday Review* on radio and television. For Gilbert Seldes's career reminds us that what highbrows write in book form has its impact on what lowbrows see, hear, or view in the newer media.

When it comes to the staples on which the great movie, radio, and television audience depends, books and the men and women who write them are as essential as cameras and cameramen, microphones and sound engineers, actors, actresses, directors, and even reporters, commentators, and newscasters. Books and authors, magazines and editors, newspapers and reporters existed centuries before the practitioners of the newer photographic arts and electronic sciences came along, and could go on existing—though, let's admit it, with diminished influence and income—if the movie, radio, and television industries all vanished from the face of the earth. But movies, radio, and television could never have commanded their present influence or piled up their past earnings if they had not been able to draw upon the books that our libraries have preserved from earlier times and from the experience and talents of our contemporary authors.

Let me cite just a few representative examples. *Gone With The Wind,* the best-selling American novel of the twentieth century, also became its most profitable motion picture. The plays of Shakespeare and of Shaw have provided the screen with several of its outstanding masterpieces. Movie script-writers, directors, and actors have translated the novels of Tolstoy, Dostoevsky, Dickens, Melville, Dreiser, and Hemingway into film classics which will gradually become available to television audiences, too. Radio, with its exclusive reliance upon sound, now depends more on the classics of music than on the classics of literature. But as a means of reporting and interpreting news, as an outlet for discussion and debate, radio provides an unrivalled channel for swift, spontaneous, and searching transmission of ideas. The phonograph industry which once relied so heavily on the most trivial and degraded types of popular music now finds that classical records comprise about one third of all its sales: a growing, solvent, and responsive audience as the radio industry is now learning the hard and costly way.

MAGAZINES

When the great British classical scholar Sir Gilbert Murray visited the United States during the early 1920's, he asked what popular magazine had the widest circulation. When told that the *Saturday Evening Post* then had a circulation of more than 2 million copies a week, he commented: "It must be *very* bad." The recent vogue of *Confidential* magazine does not encourage those who pin their hopes on human perfectibility or the century of the common man. But as Russell Lynes, one of our foremost historians of contemporary culture has noted, such popular magazines of the present day as *Life, Look,* and *Reader's Digest,* are now publishing the kind of material that could not have been found, thirty years ago, outside such quality magazines as *Harper's* and the *Atlantic Monthly.* And while some readers find the *Digest* almost too digestible, others complain that the *New Yorker* has lost some of its bite, *Harper's* and the *Atlantic* some of their daring, the *Partisan Review* some of its defiance. But the fault here does not lie with the editors of these magazines, with their contributors, or even with their readers. The fault lies with the time in which we live—a time in which the critic, the historian, and the biographer flourish more than do the poet, the novelist, or the dramatist. In journalism it is the age of the reporter rather than the reformer, of the documentary rather than the pronunciamento.

Our cultural climate affects all those who express themselves, whether to the masses or the classes, whether in fact or fiction, whether as entertainers or educators. Because of the two world wars through which we have passed plus two postwar booms, one world depression, and now the cold war, the spirit of adventure, experiment, and revolt runs low, especially among the practitioners of the public arts who try to attract and hold the great audience. For that reason the authors, publishers, and purveyors of books bear a special responsibility—all the more so because the times are not propitious to the kind of original writing and thinking which they and they alone produce. Just this spring, half a dozen critics have come upon half a dozen new novelists for whom they predict great things. Maybe so. But as one who has had a casual acquaintance with the book publishing industry, I fear the worst for these young writers—and the greater their talents, the more dread their prospects. For I cannot think of many American authors—especially the authors of novels—

who do not receive more from their movie, television, magazine, reprint, and even radio rights than from the royalties they earn from the trade editions of the books on which this whole superstructure rests. And yet the author who does not devote the major part of his time to writing books eventually finds his income from so-called subsidiary rights drying up, along with his reputation and self-esteem.

These remarks apply more to the writers of fiction than of nonfiction. Indeed, the nonfiction writer presents another paradox as striking as the paradox of the successful novelist who makes more money from the movie and television rights than from royalties. For the decisive books of this, or any other time, are not necessarily works of fiction. Most of the world's decisive books deal with ideas.

I cannot think of any single writer whose books have had greater influence on our recent past than the late Lord Keynes. The author of *The Economic Consequneces of the Peace,* published in 1920, and of *The General Theory of Employment, Interest, and Money,* published in 1936, was not a professional or full-time writer but an economist. Yet his slender, widely-read account of the Paris Peace Conference changed the thinking of a whole generation on the causes and consequences of the first World War as his lengthy, abstruse analysis of the causes of the Great Depression created the greatest revolution in economic thinking since the appearance of an even duller and heavier book, *Capital,* by Karl Marx. For when it comes to forming and changing the minds of men, no motion picture, radio program, or telecast can wield such influence as a book. For example, we are now celebrating this year's Liberty and Justice Awards, in the field of history and biography to Herbert Feis's *Churchill, Roosevelt, and Stalin.* That book will not only influence generations of scholars and students who will find in it an unrivalled account of some of the greatest events of our time. The researches of Herbert Feis will influence yet other scholars and writers and through them become part of our national heritage. And I shall be surprised if next year this same gathering is not paying similar honor to a book that has just appeared, *The*

Affluent Society by John Kenneth Galbraith, which seems likely to affect the economic thought of our time as profoundly as Keynes influenced the economic thought of the 1930's.

Although the publishers of the Feis and Galbraith books will never get rich through the motion picture, radio, or television rights, the ideas those books set forth will reach television and radio audiences directly and at once, movie audiences indirectly and eventually. For radio and television do bring ideas to the American people through programs of news, discussion, and public service. . . .

Today's radio and television commentators—like the industries they serve—transmit but do not originate ideas and opinions. . . . Those of us who report, interpret, or analyze news on radio or television; those of us who try to reach any part of that great radio-television audience depend more on the books we read and have read than on any other source of information and inspiration. I should add, for my own part, I depend more on books than on all other sources combined.

The essential, distinctive purpose of radio and television is to transmit ideas and impressions; not to create them. The essential, distinctive purpose of the book industry is to originate and develop literary talent; not to merchandise its products. Of course, the radio, and television industries do not reject new ideas or original talents. Neither does the book publisher deliberately reject or sabotage best-sellers. . . . Just as it is to the interest of the book industry that radio and television should prosper, so it is to the interest of radio and television that the book come up with new talents, new ideas, new material which will be transformed and worked over into radio broadcasts, and television productions. It is from the world of books that these newer industries have drawn the bulk of their inspiration; it is also from these newer industries that books, authors, and publishers increasingly depend for economic survival.

The book industry, during the past ten years, has greatly increased its revenues and its public through the development of the paperback book and the cultivation of newsstands and drugstore counters as channels of distribution. Because our public libraries have so long played so large a part in bringing books to the general public, their role has perhaps been taken for granted. But the motion picture, radio, and television industries fail to bring their growing audiences better and better material insofar as they pay less and less attention to quality. The book industry, on the other hand, has laid increasing stress on the size of its audience without sacrificing the quality of the product. . . .

The chief problem of the book industry is economic. Publishers do not lack for titles or authors for themes. Nor does the publisher restrict the author's freedom of expression any more than the government or any third party restricts the freedom of the publisher to issue whatever books he pleases, within the limits of the laws, of libel, slander, and obscenity. The problem of the author and publisher is to find a large enough public for their books to make their joint enterprise worthwhile. If it were not for our libraries, many of the books that now appear would never see the light of day and those that do appear would have far less influence and readership. In some instances, this can even prove a danger to the public peace. Just before Manuel Azana, the president of Madrid's leading literary club, became the first president of the Spanish Republic, the great philosopher Unamuno gave voice to this humorous warning:

Beware of Azana. He is an author without readers who would be capable of starting a revolution to be read.

The traditional freedoms guaranteed by the Bill of Rights deal chiefly with the rights of those who communicate with the public rather than with the rights of the public to which the communication is directed. The United States Postal and Customs authorities, certain state censorship boards, and some local police officials still   place occasional restrictions on free speech and expression. The motion picture, radio, and television industries police themselves. Because they seek so large an audience they voluntarily limit their own freedom of expression rather than risk offending substantial minorities. But it has remained for the television industry to restrict the variety of the material it broadcasts to the same degree that it widens its audience. Partly this reflects the fear of the television industry that it will antagonize any part of its great audience. But it goes deeper than that. The moment the television industry subordinates its concern for the great audience to a concern for any part of that audience, it courts immediate and total bankruptcy just as surely as does the book publisher who takes the opposite course and subordinates his concern for an infinite variety of specialized audiences to a concern for the great audience.

It does not follow from this that the book publisher must content himself forever with publishing for a thousand little coteries or that television—the most public, at the moment, of the public arts—must try to find ways and means of placing still more restrictions on its programs. But if these two vicious cycles are to be broken, the initiative must come from the book industry which has had long experience in a manageable field rather than from the television industry which has had brief experience in an unmanageable one. And both the long-established book industry and the more newly established television industry can learn much from our librarians who have had far longer experience than either in a field as wide as human experience itself.

For our libraries and librarians offer living proof of the vitality of liberty—liberty, that is, to collect, to treasure, and to make available every kind of written record the human race has left during its brief history on this small planet. The book publisher can no more afford to publish books with the freedom that a library collects them than a television network can afford to broadcast material with the freedom that a publisher issues it in book form. But as long as our libraries enjoy and exercise complete freedom to gather and circulate books and as long as our book publishers enjoy and exercise complete freedom to issue and distribute books, it will be up to our scholars, poets, novelists, and historians to sustain our distinctive culture of the book. And as long as that culture remains alive and available, it is up to the public arts to pass it on, as best they can to wider audiences.

The new public arts have already drawn heavily on the talents of actors, musicians, artists, dancers, and writers as well as on the skills of scientists and technicians. In the motion picture we are witnessing the emergence of a new and unique art form, but radio and television have achieved their greatest triumphs when they have transmitted great music and great musicians, great dramas and great actors to the great audience. Television has not yet produced any great talents itself; when NBC broadcast its series of the wise men, it included three poets: Robert Frost, Carl Sandburg, and John Hall Wheelock—men who had devoted their lives to the world of books.

If none of the public arts has yet produced a wise man of its own, that's because the highest function of the public arts is not to create but to transmit greatness. And if the public arts have let the public down, it is not because the public arts have brought forth no greatness of their own; it is because they make inadequate use of the greatness already at their disposal. What the public arts have done that they ought not to have done, what they have left undone that they ought to have done, it is not for me, or any outsider, to say. But it does not take any inside insight to recognize that the public arts, especially television, have let us down because of their inadequate channels of public communication, not because they lack the material to communicate or the skill to establish contact with the audience. And while our authors and publishers, our booksellers and librarians reach all too small a proportion of their great potential audience, their failure is not due to any lack of richness or variety in the wares they offer. Their failure is due to a lack of audience.

With the public arts it's just the other way around. For while the public arts reach a vast mass audience, they squander their marvelous skills and techniques on meager and monotonous material. The not-so-great reading public enjoys the widest choice of what it may read or leave unread. The infinitely greater television public enjoys only the narrowest choice of what it may view or turn off.

I hope I have posed the problem in such a way that

librarians will recognize their unique role. In so far as any of us can transcend ourselves and our callings we may be able to break new ground, especially if we remember the wisdom of Winston Churchill who once said courage is rightly esteemed the first of human qualities because it is the one that guarantees all the others. □

PREAMBLE

Convinced that books remain essential tools for preserving and diffusing the world's storehouse of knowledge;

Believing that the role of books can be reinforced by the adoption of policies designed to encourage the widest possible use of the printed word;

Recalling that the Constitution of the United Nations Educational, Scientific and Cultural Organization calls for the promotion of "the free flow of ideas by word and image" as well as "international co-operation calculated to give the people of all countries access to the printed and published materials produced by any of them";

Recalling further that the General Conference of Unesco has affirmed that books "perform a fundamental function in the realization of Unesco's objectives, namely peace, development, the promotion of human rights and the campaign against racialism and colonialism";

Considering that the General Conference of Unesco has proclaimed 1972 International Book Year, with the theme "Books for All";

the

International Community of Booksellers Associations

Reprinted by permission of the U.S. Secretariat, International Book Year, 1972, Esther J. Walls, Director.

International Confederation of Societies of Authors and
   Composers
International Federation for Documentation
International Federation of Library Associations
International Federation of Translators
International PEN
International Publishers Association

Adopt unanimously this Charter of the Book, and call upon
all concerned to give effect to the principles here enunciated.

ARTICLE I

Everyone has the right to read

Society has an obligation to ensure that everyone has an opportunity to enjoy the benefit of reading. Since vast portions
of the world's population are deprived of access to books by
inability to read, governments have the responsibility of helping to obliterate the scourge of illiteracy. They should encourage provision of the printed materials needed to build
and maintain the skill of reading. Bilateral and multilateral
assistance should be made available, as required, to the book
professions. The producers and distributors of books, for
their part, have the obligation to ensure that the ideas and information thus conveyed continue to meet the changing
needs of the reader and of society as a whole.

ARTICLE II

Books are essential to education

In an era of revolutionary changes in education and far-reaching programmes for expanded school enrollment, planning is
required to ensure an adequate textbook component for the
development of educational systems. The quality and content
of educational books need constant improvement in all countries of the world. Regional production can assist national
publishers in meeting requirements for textbooks as well as
for general educational reading materials which are particularly needed in school libraries and literacy programmes.

ARTICLE III

*Society has a special obligation to establish
the conditions in which authors can
exercise their creative role*

The Universal Declaration of Human Rights states that
"everyone has the right to the protection of the moral and
material interests resulting from any scientific, literary or artistic production of which he is the author". This protection
should be also extended to translators, whose work opens the
horizons of a book beyond linguistic frontiers, thus providing
an essential link between authors and a wider public. All
countries have the right to express their cultural individuality
and in so doing preserve the diversity essential to civilization.
Accordingly they should encourage authors in their creative
role and should through translation provide wider access to
the riches contained in the literature of other languages, including those of limited diffusion.

ARTICLE IV

*A sound publishing industry is essential
to national development*

In a world in which there are sharp disparities in book production, with many countries lacking adequate reading materials, it is necessary to plan for the development of national
publishing. This requires national initiative and, where necessary, international co-operation to help create the infrastructure needed. The development of publishing industries also
entails integration with education and economic and social
planning; the participation of professional organizations, ex-
tending in so far as possible across the entire book community through institutions such as national book development
councils; and long-term, low interest financing on a national,
bilateral or multilateral basis.

ARTICLE V

*Book manufacturing facilities are necessary
to the development of publishing*

In their economic policies, governments should ensure that necessary supplies and equipment are available for the development of an infrastructure for book manufacture, including paper, printing and binding machinery. The maximum use of national resources, together with eased importation of these supplies and equipment, will promote the production of inexpensive and attractive reading materials. Urgent attention should also be given to the development of transcriptions of oral languages. Those concerned with the manufacture of books should maintain the highest practicable standards of production and design. Particular efforts should be made for the manufacture of books for the handicapped.

ARTICLE VI

*Booksellers provide a fundamental service as a link
between publishers and the reading public*

In the forefront of efforts to promote the reading habit, booksellers have both cultural and educational responsibilities. They play a vital role in ensuring that an adequate and well-chosen range of books reaches the reading public. Special book post and air freight rates, payment facilities and other financial incentives aid them in carrying out this function.

ARTICLE VII

*Libraries are national resources for the transfer
of information and knowledge, for the
enjoyment of wisdom and beauty*

Libraries occupy a central position in the distribution of books. They are often the most effective means of getting printed matter to the reader. As a public service, they promote reading which, in turn, advances individual well-being, life-long education and economic and social progress. Library services should correspond to each nation's potentialities and needs. Not only in cities, but especially in the vast rural areas which frequently lack book supplies, each school and each community should possess at least one library with qualified staff and an adequate book budget. Libraries are also essential for higher education and scholarly requirements. The development of national library networks will enable readers everywhere to have access to book resources.

ARTICLE VIII

Documentation serves books by preserving and making available essential background material

Scientific, technical and other specialized books require adequate documentation services. Accordingly, such services should be developed, with the assistance of governments and all elements of the book community. In order that maximum information materials may be available at all times, measures should be taken to encourage the freest possible circulation across frontiers of these essential tools.

ARTICLE IX

The free flow of books between countries is an essential supplement to national supplies and promotes international understanding

To enable all to share in the world's creativity, the unhampered flow of books is vital. Obstacles such as tariffs and taxes can be eliminated through widespread application of Unesco agreements and other international recommendations and treaties. Licenses and foreign currency for the purchase of books and the raw materials for book-making should be accorded generally, and internal taxes and other restraints on trade in books reduced to a minimum.

ARTICLE X

*Books serve international understanding
and peaceful co-operation*

"Since wars begin in the minds of men", the Unesco Constitution states, "it is in the minds of men that the defences of peace must be constructed". Books constitute one of the major defences of peace because of their enormous influence in creating an intellectual climate of friendship and mutual understanding. All those concerned have an obligation to ensure that the content of books promotes individual fulfillment, social and economic progress, international understanding and peace.

Approved at Brussels,
22 October 1971,
by the Support Committee for
International Book Year.

LIBRARIANS

AND

LIBRARIANSHIP

SALUTE TO LIBRARIANS

Catherine Drinker Bowen

The pleasing condition known as true love is seldom attained without difficulty. Nowadays, I can declare with truth that I am in love with librarians—engaged in a perpetual, delightful affair of the heart with all public custodians of books.

But in my early twenties, struggling in library basements with bound volumes of newspapers or shuffling through a jungle of card catalogues, I was convinced that librarians existed solely to keep people from reading books. It is natural for young readers to experience shyness in big city or university libraries; the presence of so many books is at the same time exciting and intimidating. The young scholar longs for introduction, a knowledgeable hand to reach, point, act as intermediary between himself and all those riches.

In early days, I tried not to give librarians any trouble, which was where I made my primary mistake. Librarians like to be given trouble; they exist for it, they are geared to it. For the location of a mislaid volume, an uncatalogued item, your good librarian has a ferret's nose. Give her a scent and she jumps the leash, her eye bright with battle. But I did not know this. All unaware I used to make my way to those block-long municipal buildings, hope in my heart and in my

hand a list of ten or fifteen books. Not books to read in the
library but to take home, where I could copy at length, with
time to think about what I was copying. I did not telephone
beforehand and ask to have my books ready at the desk. I
took my list and looked up the proper numbers in the card
catalogue, rechecked each one and carried the cards to the
desk. The young woman would glance at the cards and then
she would say, "Only two books at a time can be taken from
the circulation department, miss." Black hatred would then
well up in a heart that had been ready to love.

"Shut not your doors to me proud libraries." Walt Whitman had said it and the words gave comfort, letting me know
the great had their troubles, too, in libraries. But I was puzzled. Why should there be a conspiracy to keep anyone away
from books? The fault must lie in myself, perhaps in my lack
of systematized training in research. This was long before I
had met the professors or attended a conference of historians;
there was still fixed in my mind the pleasing illusion that the
possessor of a Ph.D. in history has before him a blazed trail, a
path straight to the heart of his subject.

While I was working on the life of Tchaikovsky, in 1938,
a British musicologist happened to be a guest in my brother's
house. I admired Professor Dent's books about musicians; I
was sure that so famous a scholar could tell me how to proceed and that his experience would provide a magic formula
for libraries, an open sesame to those tall imperious doors. I
asked Mr. Dent point-blank how he went about his research.
(I was too inexperienced to know this is not a question one
asks of scholars.) "Do you use five-by-eight cards?" I said.
"How do you start, for instance?"

Mr. Dent smiled. "How do *you* start?" he asked. "How
do you do your research?"

"Me?" I said. "Oh, I just plunge around in libraries."

Twenty-three years and five books later, I know that
Mr. Dent answered me in the only way he could. On that
tortuous long journey there is indeed no sure trail, no short-
cut. I went ahead, plunging and bucking my way through libraries or slinking defeated from some municipal encounter.

I do not know how it is with other students of history. But looking back, it seems my every forward movement derived not from success but failure, from some humiliation suffered, inducing anger, the stubborn resolve to find what I knew was on the shelves and use it in my own way for better or for worse.

One day in the New York Public Library, I received a crushing rebuff. That the incident was due to my own ineptitude made it, as usual, no easier to bear. I had walked into the Slavonic Division and told the learned curator that I was writing a life of Tchaikovsky. Might I look around, not at the cards but at the shelved books, the titles? "You speak Russian, of course?" the curator asked, with a fine roll of the R. His question took me by surprise. Actually, I knew enough to read titles and find my way about. But I gave a cautious negative. No, I didn't speak the language.

The curator shrugged. "No Russian?" he said. "Then of what use to come to this room? What use to write a life of Peter Ilich Tchaikovsky?"

I turned tail and fled, too flustered to stop and explain that I had a Russian collaborator, and that we both knew quite well what we were doing. At the Pennsylvania Station I boarded the train for home. By the time we reached Princeton Junction I had recovered. People, I thought, should be thrusting books at me, not snatching them away! Moreover, it was high time I did something to resolve this feud between me and the charge-out ladies and gentlemen behind the desks. The train pulled into North Philadelphia, and it came to me with a redeeming flash that what I needed to study was not books, systems, "disciplines," but *librarians*.

I bought a large notebook, something I am apt to do in moments of stress. Perhaps every student does it; a clean, untouched notebook invites the bravest plans. On the outside of this one I wrote "Librarians and Libraries," and then I began making lists of the librarians I had encountered. After each name I wrote a brief and useful characterization. The lists were continued for years, they were made in all seriousness, meant only for business, and they far overflowed that first notebook. I have them today and reproduce some samples, unchanged except for the exclusion of one proper name:

Library of Congress. Mr. Shaw — Mr. Cole. Can find anything. God's sakes don't forget your library number.

Harvard Archives. Mr. Lovett, wears glasses. Bright. Mr. Elkins, seventh floor, Widener. Head Man. Cannot understand what I am trying to do but helpful. Said, "You don't want *printed* material, do you?" No use telling him why I want it. Just give him the numbers.

Widener Library downstairs. Mr. X . . . Old curmudgeon. Hates women. Keep away from him. Find out name the little short one, desk, head of stairs. Sweet.

Massachusetts Historical Society. Mrs. Hitchcock, the nice one who knows Mr. Henry Adams. When he comes in the basement she will notify me upstairs. Says better not let him catch me downstairs near the Adams Papers. Says he takes off his hearing aid to make it harder. Says don't be put down by this. Says just yell.

This last was written in the late 1940's, before the Adams Papers, a superb repository of historical material, were thrown open to scholars. Mr. Henry Adams was custodian of the Papers, and only an occasional favored student was permitted a glimpse inside the room. Mr. Barnes's famous arcanum of paintings, near Philadelphia, was never more difficult to penetrate; I was forewarned to failure. Already there had been correspondence by mail and by messenger. At Mr. Adams's instance I had reduced my requests to specific queries. There were eight of these, carefully worded and typed; I had delivered them to Mr. Adams's office on State Street. What I wanted from the Adams Papers was modest enough; it had to do with John Adams at college, between 1751 and 1755. Adams's *Autobiography* had been printed nearly a century ago in what its editor called "fragments," opening with the year 1775; the Massachusetts Historical Society had printed a brief and still earlier "fragment" in which John Adams told of taking his entrance examinations

for Harvard. It seemed to me there must be more, somewhere. Adams was deeply interested in education. Surely he
would mention his teachers, his tutors? I counted on one
more meeting with the curator of the Papers, here in the Historical Society. A last chance and I knew it.

I had been at work in the library for perhaps a week,
when one morning Mrs. Hitchcock sent word that Mr. Henry
Adams had entered the building and was on his way up in the
elevator. The second floor of the Massachusetts Historical
Society is a succession of handsome, open rooms that echo,
with lofty doorways and marble floors. I stood perhaps ten
steps from the elevator. Mr. Adams got out, took a startled
look at me and snatched a hearing button from each ear. My
instinct was for retreat but I advanced, and there in the open
room gave tongue for a full half-hour. Mr. Adams had my list;
I had a carbon. We stood and I shouted. Finally Mr. Adams
seized me by the elbow. "Mrs. Bowen," he said, "I don't
want to block your work. I don't want to be the cause of
destroying your chapters, as you say I will. But you cannot
have this material. It has never been printed. You know very
well it has never been printed. *How do you know it is in the
Adams Papers?"*

I told Mr. Adams I did not know, but that I had studied
his ancestor for a long time, and such studies permitted one
to infer that John Adams might have mentioned these matters in his *Autobiography*. I said that inference was the business of a biographer.

Mr. Adams's voice rose to a pitch of real distress. "Mrs.
Bowen," he said, "I wish I had never laid *eyes* on you."

Something in the desperate pronunciation of the noun
softened me; plainly, Mr. Adams's suffering was worse than
mine. I gave up and we parted in a mutual rush. Downstairs in
the little retiring room I threw myself on the couch; the
sound of my voice still rang in my ears. The entire Historical
Society had been apprised of my work, hopes, ambitions;
right now I desired nothing so much as dignified anonymity.
A Japanese girl was standing by the mirror, arranging her hair.
"Excuse me," she said, "but are you writing a life of John
Adams?"

I told the young woman she must know that, by now. Everyone in the building must know it.

She smiled politely, but her next words startled me. "What was the old gentleman afraid of?" she said.

I went home to Philadelphia and fidgeted. How could I complete my chapter without that material? I was genuinely worried, in a condition of frustration, and I could not proceed. At the end of three weeks, on the day before Christmas, an envelope came in the mail, postmarked Boston. Inside, typed laboriously by Mr. Adams, was everything I had asked for. Plainly, he had entered that sacred room, had found what I wanted, taken it down, and copied it line for line. What alchemy melted his New England heart I do not know. I know only that a surge of relief and joy came over me; I can feel it now, some ten years afterward.

Since those hazardous days, matters have begun to run smoothly for me in libraries. Confronted by fifty thousand books I have not lost my diffidence; perhaps it has increased. But I am not at all abashed in the presence of librarians. I can remember the day the tide began to turn. It was in the Pennsylvania Historical Society, at Thirteenth and Locust Streets, in Philadelphia. I was three-quarters through my life of John Adams and needed some eighteenth-century broadsides to brighten my chapters on the Continental Congress. Research for my preceeding book, on Justice Holmes, had been done in Boston and Washington; I was unfamiliar with the Pennsylvania Historical Society and no one there knew me. I walked into the building and upstairs to the library, signed my name in the ledger and went to the card catalogues by the window.

I had not gone through the A's when I felt a tap on my shoulder, and the librarian from the desk handed me a folded slip of paper. It was a note from the director, Richard Norris Williams. "Mrs. Bowen," it said, "would you like a quiet room to work in upstairs?"

I kept that message tacked above my desk for weeks. It cheered me, though I had not accepted Dr. Williams's kind offer because I like the genial commotion of the card catalogue room, the companionship of other readers and the nearness of the books. In research libraries, one hesitancy remained, however, to plague me. It was brought on by the repeated question, put to me first by Mr. Elkins on the seventh floor of the Widener Library: "You don't want *printed* material, do you?" That query, always phrased negatively by research librarians, still had power to put me down. Yet even this bogy was shortly due for exorcism. Again, I recall the day.

Because he is hunting for detail, the biographer finds his material, as I have said, in unlikely places, and this is true in libraries as well as in personal interviews or an out-of-door search conducted through the subject's home county or locale. Suppose one wants to find who was proprietor of a certain Philadelphia tavern, favored by John Adams in a hot July of 1775. The matter may be concealed in some quite ordinary volume, say the published memoirs of a cousin thrice removed, or in scattered notes on Philadelphia streets, compiled in the mid-nineteenth century by some finicky antiquarian and printed obscurely at his own expense.

A list of such publications is not impressive to scholars, accustomed as they are to primary or manuscript sources, and I was conscious of it. The incident that liberated me took place in the Free Library of Philadelphia. It began on that vast second floor, where I had gone to check my book numbers, carrying in my hand a list of just such titles as I have described — thirteen of them, each referring to material vital to my subject and discovered by me at the cost of much time and digging.

I had never used this public library, but the general reference collection is large and it seemed likely the volumes would be here, rather than in a more specialized collection. I found my numbers in the cards and took them to the librarian at the circulation desk. "Only two books at a time . . ." she began.

Two blades of grass to a cow, I told myself, would be as nourishing. I left my books on the desk and wandered off. In libraries it is not well to hurry. To the research worker, haste is fatal. The books have been where they are for a long time; they reveal themselves slowly, at their own pace.

Drifting downstairs in search of help, I came upon a door marked *Assistant Librarian in Charge of Research.* For a public library it was an odd, inviting title. I knocked and walked into a big square room, littered from floor almost to ceiling with the tools of the working scholar: bibliographies, dictionaries, encyclopedias, rare book catalogues, and un-answered letters, no doubt from other librarians.

A young man with startling white hair rose from a table where he was writing. I told him my name and what had oc-curred upstairs. He seized my hand and wrung it, said I could have anything I wanted in the library, took my list, ran an eye over it, and remarked, all in one loud welcoming breath, "Trash! Everything on this list is trash. My name is John Powell. What do you want with third-rate books like these?" — and was on the intercom telephone to start the wheels rolling.

It was the beginning of a lasting friendship. With this young man I could defend myself, and did. How dared a li-brarian condemn the contents of books he had not read! — I demanded vigorously. These volumes contained letters print-ed nowhere else, notes from John Adams's daughter to her mother: "I have dined at General Knox's; the General is not half so fat as he was." John Powell was himself a biographer; when the books came he looked into them and made hand-some retraction, adding that there is indeed no material the biographer can afford to ignore, whether primary, tertiary or quinquagintal.

History withholds so much! Thomas Carlyle has said it with his usual violence and the hammering of his bold Ger-manic capitalizations. "Listening from a distance of Two Centuries, across the Death-chasms and the howling kingdoms of Decay, it is not easy to catch everything."

To catch everything? It is not easy to catch anything at all, or at least anything that will communicate in living terms across the centuries. The biographer is much in the position

of a journalist who looks for news. Not for fillers or musty
historical chestnuts that can be found in the textbooks, but
for *biographical news.* Sometimes the biographer's news is
gleaned from the mere titles of books. I well remember the
summer morning when first I saw the Holmes family library.
The books had recently been moved to the Library of Congress, in Washington, and awaited settlement of Justice
Holmes's will before being catalogued and arranged. A young
librarian, shirt-sleeved against the heat, took me upstairs in a
small staff elevator, led me down a corridor, unlocked a door
and beckoned me into a narrow, steel-walled room.

Stored and filed on shelves, tables, chairs, were the accumulated personal libraries of three generations of Holmeses,
some six thousand volumes in all. Perhaps half were law-
books; they filled two rooms; yellow library slips stuck out
from the pages. Framed pictures, tied in stacks, lay along the
floor and there was a wooden box of china, each piece wrap-
ped in tissue paper. At the door a table held a pile of dime
thrillers in paper back, with lurid drama depicted on the
covers; I wondered if they belonged here and which of the
family had collected them.

Altogether it was an inspiring, dazzling, dusty sight.
Here were books beloved of Wendells, Olivers, Jacksons,
Holmeses, inscribed on flyleaves by donors and owners:
"O. W. H. Jr., from his loving father and mother, Christmas,
1859." Here were Dr. Holmes's books on music, acquired no
doubt when he was learning to play the violin in the 1850's.
(A trying time for the family; the good Doctor considered
fiddle playing to be a mere matter of time and application.) I
noted the German edition of his *Autocrat of the Breakfast
Table . . . Der Tisch-despot.* What a travesty of a title, and
how had the Doctor felt when first he saw it?

Here were books I had myself been reared on: *The Dolly
Dialogues,* Anstey's *Tinted Venus,* the many volumes of old
Isaac D'Israeli's *Curiosities of Literature.* There were enough
Latin books to stock a school — Mr. Epes Sargent Dixwell's
own school, no doubt, where O. W. Holmes, Jr., had studied.
And here was Mr. Dixwell's *Phaedrus,* with a signed photo-

graph of William Tyndall pasted in, dated 1877. Here also were the *Letters to a Young Physician, Just Entering upon Practice,* by James Jackson, M.D., L.L.D. That would be Justice Holmes's grandfather, I thought, through the maternal line; he had dedicated his book to that excellent physician, Dr. John C. Warren, Professor of Anatomy at Harvard. There was a chapter on "Somnambulism, Animal Magnetism and Insanity"; there was one on "Phthises" which recommended exercise in the open air, particularly horseback riding. The chapter "On Dyspepsy" went direct to the point: "I believe that very many persons are benefitted from the juice of the grape, and I choose to say so. I love to tell the truth, even when it is unfashionable."

What a very sensible book, I told myself, and copied the sentences in my notes. "On entering the sick room," wrote Dr. Jackson, "the physician's deportment should be calm, sober without solemnity, civil without formality. He should abstain from all levity. He should never attract attention to himself. He should leave the room with an air of cheerfulness. . . ."

During all this time, the librarian had waited, sitting on a box by the door. I paused in my reading to tell him a person could learn more about the Holmeses, here in this little room, than in a dozen interviews with the Justice's friends and relatives. The librarian asked how long I expected to stay. "All day," I said. The librarian replied that he would have to stay with me; readers were not permitted in this room by themselves. I said I was sorry to take up his time. Following my usual procedure I opened my briefcase, took out paper and a dozen sharpened pencils and laid them conveniently by. Then I removed my hat and shoulder bag, produced from the latter a kitchen apron (library dust can begrime one's traveling clothes), and put it on.

The librarian watched. Then he smiled. "I think the library can assume this risk," he said quietly, and took his departure.

I never saw him again. But I remember that young man with gratitude. He led me where I wanted to go and showed me what I had come there to see, then took my measure and left me with the books.

Recently I heard a young lawyer say, "When I go into a really good library, things happen to me." For the librarians there could be no tastier compliment and none more true. Since I began to read in libraries some thirty years ago, times have changed and policies have altered. Modern librarians look on it as their business to make their shelves inviting. A librarian's policy depends, of course, on where he is placed. Among rare books, custodial care is of first importance, whereas in the public libraries of great cities it is important to "get the titles off the shelves," whether or no the volumes fall apart from overwork.

But to the biographer, a scholarly librarian stands at times in the relation of editor. By tactful approach the librarian will discover the scheme of one's book, how widely one plans to explore certain phases of history, certain scenes and personalities. What he says can encourage expansion, a deeper treatment. He calls on the telephone or writes letters at strategic moments: "We are on the trail of that holograph map [or that portrait or manuscript letter]. We have written twice to England and enclose replies to date. We will surely track this item down. By the way, last night our Miss Y. found that 1607 edition of Cowell's *Interpreter*. Do you still want to take it home? . . . May we say your treatment of the Norwich episode is especially valuable and we hope you will not give up but pursue it further."

In the five or six years it takes to write a biography, such expert, persistent interest is to the writer like food to the famished. The librarian has gone beyond the path of duty; he believes in one's book and his involvement proves it. For lack of certain material, the biographer may have deleted a telling episode. But the librarian's letter gives the writer heart. He fishes his chapter from the pile, inserts a blank page on which he scribbles, *Librarian X will supply material,* and arranges his narrative accordingly.

As it happens, I am especially dependent on librarians

because my scheme of biography requires that I do the entire bulk of reading myself. Contrary to common practice, I do not engage research workers to go to libraries and read for me, or even to search for specific things. Such a helper, no matter how skillfully trained, may miss something on the way, some side picture, name or incident vital to the illumination of my characters. Therefore I prefer to make the journey alone, though it may add years to my task.

I have known librarians over half the world. I think their praises are not often sung, and I am glad to sing them now. Wherever they are, I salute them and wish them joy of their work.   □

THE ELEMENTS OF A GOOD LIBRARIAN

Lawrence Clark Powell

After thirty-four years of giving out and getting in books, UCLA's head circulation librarian retired. Most of those years and for seven days a week this strong woman was on her feet, making fast connections between books and people and keeping her files nailed, and her sense of humor.

A few years ago, before going to an American Library Association Conference, I planned to inverview an applicant for a loan desk position, and so I asked Deborah King what to look for.

"Good feet," was all she said.

Are there any other elements of a good librarian? A paragon might be formed as follows:

A good librarian is energetic. (I get lazier as I grow older, and want to dream more and do less.)

A good librarian is honest. (I once stole a book and sneaked it back in, when my first job was in the library from which I had taken the book ten years before.)

A good librarian has an encyclopedic mind. (I flunked geometry, had a hard time with French, got a C in cataloguing, and never could deal with Dewey.)

A good librarian is selfless. (I have always had to fight against being self-centered.)

> *A good librarian is patient.* (I have a do-it-now compulsion which is shortening my life and those of the people around me who have not learned how to protect themselves.)
> *A good librarian is orderly.* (My desk is. At home my books are crudely classified.)
> *A good librarian is tolerant.* (I despise librarians who don't read, and people who show their slides. I also have a bad name for being bookish to the point of blindness.)

A recent visitor demonstrated to me my bad name in librarianship. As he came timidly into my office, he stopped near the door and said, "I am a documentalist." I was speechless, as he approached cautiously and sat on the edge of his chair. He was such a nice man, he almost made me ashamed of the things I have said about non-book librarians.

In short, I am a man who would be a good librarian, but who falls short because of the limitations of my own character.

I can only describe what I value most in a librarian—what I myself strive to be—and in terms of librarians whom I have seen exhibiting these elements of goodness.

One Sunday we were lunching at a neighbor's upcoast from us, an enchanting house near the sea cliff in the midst of semi-wild foliage—mesembryanthemum, sweet alyssum, rosemary, and salt bush—looking out on the waters sailed by Drake and Dana.

We were eating on trays in the living room, whose front wall was all windows and whose wall in back of where I was sitting was all books. I could feel, but not see them at my back, a thousand or more volumes reflecting the educated mind of their owner.

Politeness kept my attention on the conversation, as we ate a good meal and talked about the beaches of Baja California and the craters on the moon, about the Ponte Vecchio and the Rainbow Bridge. My left hand, however, roamed behind me over the backs of the books on the bottom shelf, practicing biblio-osmosis, and kept returning to a single book, wondering what it was, for it was taller and thinner than the rest, a modern book with a jacket, in the midst of older books in calf and cloth.

My mind became obsessed with this invisible volume and, as soon as the luncheon was over, I got up and heaved aside the overstuffed chair in which I had been sitting, dropped to my knees, and seized that tantalizing book.

It proved to be a volume of reproductions of paintings and sculptures by different artists of all periods and lands, with captions, called *The Quiet Eye, A Way of Looking at Pictures,* compiled by Sylvia Shaw Judson, and published in 1954 by Henry Regnery of Chicago.

"This book is not meant to teach," the preface said, "it is intended as an experience. The illustrations represent a long and happy search. They are admittedly the choice of one woman who is conditioned by her own life."

This Quaker woman, Sylvia Shaw Judson, who compiled *The Quiet Eye,* chose her examples to reveal a sense of "divine ordinariness, a delicate balance between the outward and the inward, with freshness and a serene wholeness and respect for all simple first-rate things, and which are for all times and all people." Pictures ranged from Dürer to Brancusi, captions from St. Augustine to Aldous Huxley.

She achieved her aim. The effect on me was that of an experience. I was not the same for having looked at and read it. It cleared and deepened my vision. The caption for a picture by Henri Rousseau set me on a path I had not walked since boyhood. It read: "All things were new; and all the creation gave another smell unto me than before, beyond what words can utter."

The words are those of George Fox, founder of the Society of Friends, who lived from 1644 to 1691. They are from his Journal, published three years after his death.

When we had returned home, I went to my study and laid hands on an old book which had been a family fixture since boyhood and to which I had become so accustomed that I never saw it, even when my eyes were on it.

Looking at Sylvia Judson's *The Quiet Eye* cleared my cloudy vision, and I spent that evening reading in this family

copy of the first edition of George Fox's Journal, an ancient
book bearing the successive signatures of my forebears who in
turn had owned it.

This led to my ordering the definitive text of Fox's
Journal, published by the Cambridge University Press in
1953, and to a widening interest in the faith to which I had
been born.

A good librarian is curious.

In 1954 I dedicated my *Alchemy of Books* to Nellie
Keith, city librarian of South Pasadena during the book-
hungry years of my boyhood. The library was a wonderful
one. No one ever bothered me with "readers' advisory service." I knew what I wanted. I never wasted my time in the
children's room. My earliest reading was Grimm's grim *Fairy
Tales, Tom Sawyer,* and the *Book of Knowledge,* which I
never thought of as children's books. I liked compact books
with dense type pages, because I read fast, and those silly picture books with a few words to a page lasted about two
minutes.

I went to the library on my bicycle after dinner, first of
all to play a game called "Ditch" with my cronies, around the
library park and in and out of the library building. This we
could do with safety as long as we kept out of Mrs. Keith's
sight, for she was deaf. We used to crawl by the loan desk
from one side of the building to the other on our hands
and knees.

When exhausted from play, I would select my books and
leave. Sometimes she caught me. Then the punishment was
no books that night. Gradually she broke me out of my wild
ways, at least in the library.

I don't know a thing about Nellie Keith in the way of
her formal education for librarianship or where she had worked before she came to South Pasadena. I suspect that her
education and experience were limited. I don't even know if
she read books or knew anything about the history of libraries and learning.

And yet, Nellie Keith had at least one of the elements of
a good librarian. She was perceptive of my exceptional

reading ability, and my hunger for books was not interfered with by her annoyance at my noisy play habits. She perceived my need and she met it, and thereby unknowingly determined my ultimate fate; for, twenty years later, when Althea Warren asked me why I didn't declare for librarianship, I thought back to the first librarian I had known, and the image of Nellie Keith came before my eyes—stamping out books, with a twinkle in her eye, sending a small boy out of the building with his arms full of books.

The book stamping Nellie Keith did was clerical, but the important thing is that she carried out this task at the key point in the library, past which people came and went. And she saw them, knew them, talked with them, observed what they read, and was the symbol of service to the citizens who used the public library.

Abdicate this key position in a library to a clerk who does nothing but the charging routines, or to a machine, and you have abdicated your standing as the one who delivers more than the books.

A good librarian is perceptive.

We live in a perilous time. The advantages of mass communication are many in keeping people informed by newspaper, radio, television, films, of all that is happening everywhere every day. There is a sense of excitement and wonder engendered by the front page of the morning paper. And there is also danger in it, when pressure groups exploit these media to create public hysteria. Not only groups—single men. I was teaching at Columbia University at the time of McCarthy's heyday, and I saw what unscrupulous conduct can do to injure people.

It was a year or two before this that we saw what a single librarian allied with a journalist could do by attacking the work of a good teacher of librarians. I refer to the distorted review of Helen Haines's *Living with Books*. The index of *Library Literature* is nearly devoid of reference to this incident. The exception is the strong reply made by Elinor Earle of Akron in the *ALA Bulletin*.

I recall another case, which at the time was tentatively

considered by the American Library Association Intellectual
Freedom Committee and not dealt with because it was held
that the issues were cloudy. They are clearer now. I could not
find any reference to the case in the index of *Library Literature*. I refer to the case of Mary Knowles, librarian of the
Plymouth Monthly Meeting of the Society of Friends, in
Plymouth, Pennsylvania.

In 1953 Mrs. Knowles had been dismissed from a position in Massachusetts because in 1948 she had been a member
of an organization on the Attorney General's list of subversive groups, and would not reveal the names of associates and
was opposed in principle to loyalty oaths. In 1954 the Pennsylvania Quaker group employed her as librarian, satisfied
that she had renounced her former left-wing association and
was in fact a loyal American and a competent librarian. Both
she proved by word and deed to be.

But patriot groups and congressional investigators would
not let Mrs. Knowles's past be forgotten, and a storm of controversy was blown up and kept turbulent. The Plymouth
Meeting itself was divided, but the sense of the Meeting was
to support their appointment. When the Fund for the Republic made a grant of $5,000 to the Plymouth Meeting for its
support of democratic principles, the storm reached gale
force. In 1956 Mrs. Knowles was again called before a congressional committee and, upon her refusal to recognize the
committee's right to compel her to reveal details of past associations, was convicted of contempt of Congress.*

Whereupon, the Library Committee of Plymouth Meeting issued this public statement on January 24, 1957:

> A committee of Congress has just spent virtually a
> whole day ventilating the unhappy internal affairs of a
> small religious group, Plymouth Meeting of the Religious
> Society of Friends. Not a single fact has been developed
> that was not known before.
>
> Mrs. Knowles has sworn that she has had no subver-
> sive association since 1948, and no evidence has been

*In 1961 the United States Supreme Court reversed her conviction.

produced to the contrary. Unless, or until, evidence is produced indicating activity inimical to our democratic form of government, we envision no change in our relationship with her.

As individual members of the Religious Society of Friends, we reaffirm the supremacy of conscience. We recognize the privileges and obligations of citizenship; but we reject as false that philosophy which sets the state above moral law and demands from the individual unquestioning obedience to every state command. On the contrary, we assert that every individual, while owing loyalty to the state, owes a more binding loyalty to a higher authority—the authority of God and conscience.

In a pamphlet entitled "The Plymouth Meeting Controversy, a Report prepared for the Civil Liberties Committee of the Philadelphia Yearly Meeting of the Religious Society of Friends," we read the following:

> A basic religious issue has been raised: the Christian belief in the power of truth to unfold in every human heart and in the possibility for every person to change and develop. This implies accepting individuals for what they are at face value rather than chaining them to a past, alleged or actual.
>
> Friends' interest in these issues is rooted in long experience. From the first generation of Quakerism, Friends have been concerned to champion personal liberty and the freedom of conscience for their own members and others. Plagued in the seventeenth century by test oaths and informers, they suffered fines and imprisonment until major legal reforms were made. But in different forms the issues of religious and civil liberties rise anew in every generation.

I do not know Mrs. Knowles, either in person or by correspondence, but I do know that for a librarian to take an unpopular stand such as she took, based on principle and conscience, and to maintain it steadfastly in the face of hostility and indifference, requires the element I have been all this time leading up to.

A good librarian is courageous.

When individual courage and competence are matched
by courageous support from a librarian's board, as in this
case, the entire profession is benefited. A study of school library censorship in California, undertaken by Marjorie Fiske,
on a grant from the Fund for the Republic, and sponsored by
the University of California's School of Librarianship and the
California Library Association, was opposed at first, and Library Association support nearly caved in. The courage of
Dean J. Periam Danton, Chancellor (now President) Clark
Kerr, and Professor Frederick Mosher, chairman of the California Library Association's Intellectual Freedom Committee,
saved the day.

The results of the study, published as *School Libraries
and Censorship,* indicated that censorship in California's
school and public libraries is usually self-imposed by timid librarians who are trying to avoid controversy. They are timid
because they cannot count on the support of their professional colleagues when controversy arises.

We are haunted by the question, Are we members of a
profession or are we self-glorified housekeepers? I am suspicious of those who define professional people as those who in
doing the brainwork direct others beneath them to do the
handwork. Thus for them it is necessary to rise administra-
tively in order to achieve status professionally. The establishment of standards for positions and libraries has of course
improved the status of people and services. The trouble is
that essentially nonprofessional librarians have a way of deck-
ing themselves out in fancy standards—degrees, surveys,
charts, etc.—and proclaiming themselves as the elite.

It is the ancient matter of form versus spirit. If the desire to serve and to learn is in a person who works in a library, that person is truly a librarian, no matter what his
formal qualifications or how he is classified. The desire to
serve others is perhaps the most important of all the elements
that make up a good librarian. The desire to learn can be in-
stilled in a person. Knowledge can be acquired. Curiosity and
courage can be strengthened by example. The desire to serve
is inborn.

Take this latter quality, this desire to serve others before one's self—and there must be added to it learning and technique and psychology, and the other refinements of education, before one gets a librarian deserving of the label "professional"; one who places the needs of patrons and his profession above his own needs and the needs of his family.

I once had visits, a month apart, from the head of a library and from a clerical employee in that library's order department. The one has a Ph.D. in so-called library science, having written a dissertation on library housekeeping; the other has a B.A. Each asked a question.

The Doctor of Philosophy asked, "How is your multiple order form working?"

The Bachelor of Arts asked, "How do you stimulate faculty members to order books in areas where the library is weak?"

Which of the two is professional?

Suppose you are the head of a small library, and at closing time on a day when you are due to hurry home and take your wife to a social engagement there arrives a person who has come a distance in urgent need to use a special collection and who has been delayed by an accident. What do you do? The answer you give will tell me whether or not you are the member of a profession.

What is this element?

A good librarian is dedicated to the service of others.

To be a good servant, one must be more than a knower; one must be a believer. Believe in what? In the goodness of mankind and life on earth. He must be an optimist. And then he must believe that his work, library service, is *the* work of works. Inner belief cannot be concealed; it is outwardly visible. The students at Cambridge who tried in vain to pull George Fox off his horse shouted, as they saw his radiant face, "See, he shines, he glistens!" He was not wearing armor. George Fox wore a suit of leather.

If believing is elementary in a good librarian, then it is even more essential in one who would teach librarians. I met Miriam Tompkins only once, when I was at Columbia. She had the office next to mine, on the highest floor of the Butler Library. Soon after I had arrived, there came a knock on my door and a woman entered. I didn't know who she was, but light shone from her face as she held out her hand and said, "Welcome to Columbia. I am Miriam Tompkins." If I ever saw a believer's face, it was hers. A week later Miriam Tompkins was dead. But what she was—her belief—lives in her students, and in me, to whom she transmitted it merely by a smile and the touch of her hand.

Can beginners be taught these elements? Can young men and women be taught to be curious, perceptive, courageous, dedicated, and believing? Yes. In only one way. By example. Not by saying; by doing.

"What you are," said Emerson, "stands above you and thunders so loudly, I cannot hear what you say." Thus it is with teachers, whether they be in library schools or in libraries. It need not be only by their own example. Library history is peopled with great librarians, by those who in their deeds were curious, perceptive, courageous, and dedicated.

The study and emulation of good librarians should be the constant concern of those who would likewise be good librarians. We need more biographies of them, more histories of their works. If one is the head of a library, his is a sacred obligation to set an example to his staff. This is the hardest thing on earth to do, for it means the wearing away of one's life in trying to be a good librarian.

The good librarian sets an example just short of fanaticism. A single librarian of such stature does more to give librarianship professional status than a thousand play-it-safe and take-it-easy free-riders.

A generation ago Charles F. Lummis, newspaper editor and first Southwest booster, found himself librarian of the Los Angeles Public Library, a position he held for only five years, from 1905 to 1910, and yet in that time this fanatically dedicated little Yankee, without either library training or experience, changed the character and direction of the library. His annual reports are the most exciting library reports I have ever read.

The same generation in California also produced James L. Gillis, founder of the state-wide county library system and teacher of a band of county librarians whose dedicated zeal has never been seen again in the West. Gillis came to librarianship from the unlikely position of lobbyist with the Southern Pacific. When a new governor asked him what he wanted as his share of the patronage, Gillis chose to be State Librarian— and the rest is library history.

Every state in the Union can recall librarians who are likewise memorable in their dedication to service, and whose preparation for librarianship was unorthodox. Today's librarians in every region and town should think continually of their librarians who were truly great. They teach us by their example. Let us not follow any lesser leaders than those who went all the way, who gave their lives in the going, and who advanced librarianship along the road behind the ministry and medicine. And let us never forget that the education of a good librarian may or may not include library school training.

And finally, a favorite book of mine is called "Fischer-isms; being a sheaf of sundry and divers utterances culled from the lectures of Martin H. Fischer, professor of physiology in the University of Cincinnati," and printed privately by C. C. Thomas of Springfield and Baltimore.

Let me quote a few of these medical aphorisms in the tradition of Hippocrates; they illuminate for me what it is to be a professional person.

Unless you overwork you underwork.

Expect an early death, it will keep you busier.

The heart is the only organ that takes no rest. That is why it is so good.

A doctor must work eighteen hours a day and seven days a week. If you cannot console yourself to this, get out of the profession.

Earth, air, fire, and water are the elements of physical matter. Curiosity, perception, courage, service, and dedicated belief are the elements of a good librarian. O Lord, help us be such! □

THE NATURAL HISTORY OF THE LIBRARIAN

Hardin Craig, Jr.

It is not uncommon for a writer to say that no profession is more misunderstood than his own. This is especially true of librarianship, and the complaint is made more poignant by the doubts which have been expressed as to whether it is indeed a profession.

Actually there seems to be no reason to withhold the cachet of "profession" from the pursuit of library science. The characteristics by which one distinguishes a profession are most of them present: those engaged in a profession are usually clannish and conscious of their mutual interests; librarians cling together like bees at swarming time. A profession should have its own jargon incomprehensible to others, or at least a highly specialized vocabulary; this is undoubtedly true of librarians, although in this respect they cannot compete with the sociologists. There should be a specialized professional literature and periodicals devoted to its dissemination, and in fact there is a large body of library literature, both general and specialized.

A profession should have a code of ethics, high-minded and idealistic, although occasionally a bit snobbish and infuriating to the laity, as in the medical profession; librarians possess such a code, part written, part understood.[1] There is usually a formal post-graduate training for a profession,

Reprinted by permission from *AAUP Bulletin,* 46: 399-405, December 1960. Copyright © 1960, American Association of University Professors.

centered on the study of a body of theory and not merely the learning of techniques, with a final granting of degrees; this is also true of library science, although a few librarians slip in at the back door. In the opinion of many, there should be a sense of dedication in undertaking a profession, and its practitioners should feel that they are serving humanity and even be willing to accept comparatively low financial rewards in doing so; this is certainly true of many librarians and should be true of all.

One of the most interesting and creditable characteristics of librarians is their fierce sense of democracy. They will not tolerate, so far as they are able to prevent it, any discrimination based on color, race, religion, or sex. That women are not discriminated against is not surprising, since librarianship was one of the first professions open to and considered respectable for women.[2] Lady librarians outnumber the men at least three to one; remove the women and all libraries would have to close tomorrow.

At the national meetings, all librarians, black or white, Protestant, Jewish or Roman Catholic, are considered to be of equal importance in the eyes of God and the American Library Association; the Association will not meet in any city where hotel or dining room discrimination is practiced against any of its members. In the state associations and local meetings of the South a certain amount of segregation in the housing and feeding of members has to be accepted, but this is done with the greatest reluctance.

It will also strike an outside observer forcibly that there is no privileged class among the different types of librarians. The college and university group does not dominate the scene or the national meetings as it does, for example, in the American Historical Association. This is because the academicians have no monopoly on libraries, either quantitatively or qualitatively. One finds that public librarians, school librarians, and librarians of the special reference collections of industry, all have their prominent and active places in any national meeting or national journal; all these groups have their special sessions and publications reflecting their special interests, but on a national scale all librarians are constantly associated. Obviously this tends to make their organization larger and stronger, as well as less academic in every sense.

Similarly, the college and university side of the library profession is not dominated by the Ivy League, although the great libraries of Harvard, Columbia, and so on are held in high respect. But of the twenty largest American academic libraries, eight are in the East, nine in the Middle West, and three in the Far West; size, although not a sure guarantee of quality, is more so in the case of a book stock than of a student body. Library schools are similarly distributed, and a degree from an Eastern library school does not carry the special prestige which Eastern degrees do in some fields of college teaching.

By the same tokens, namely that the American Library Association draws its members from all parts of the field and that even college and university librarians are not culturally guided by Eastern institutions, the librarians range more widely and imaginatively in their meetings. Whereas the Modern Language Association confines itself to a few well-worn centers in the Northeast, with an occasional daring sortie as far as Chicago, so that Eastern professors will not have to leave their firesides before Christmas, librarians travel far and wide; they think nothing of meeting now in Los Angeles, now in Minneapolis, now crossing the border to Montreal, their scope limited only by the availability of hotels to accommodate the thousands who attend the meetings and by their antipathy for segregation, to which reference has already been made.

It is a dull week in library circles that sees no convention. The national body, the ALA, meets not once but twice a year. There are regional groupings, such as the Southwestern Library Association, which meet at least biennially. All states have library associations, and these meet annually. Many states, like Texas, are divided into library districts, and these divisions have their meetings too. Many communities have their local library clubs. Groups such as the Special Libraries have additional meetings of their own. Should all else fail, there are always workshops on some phase of librarianship to relieve the librarian of the tedium of independent existence, and it is not unknown for the staff of one library to pay friendly and exploratory visits to a sister institution. It is hardly necessary to remark that the committees subservient to all these organizations and conferences are only less numerous than the sands of the sea or the spawn of the codfish.

At worst, this passion for organization and for meeting together is always time-consuming and sometimes futile, and on occasion it appears almost as if there were a conspiracy to keep the individual from paying sufficient attention to his own problems. The demands upon him to engage in membership drives, to promote regional arrangements for sharing library resources, and to expand library service in underprivileged areas are very considerable. But at best, this signal characteristic of librarians denotes and promotes a wider point of view, a desire for self-improvement, and self-sacrifice in the finest sense.

Another marked characteristic of librarians, related to their democratic spirit, and stimulated by their fondness for gathering together for discussions of all sorts, is that they are extremely sensitive to public opinion and are constantly seeking for improvement in their procedures and techniques. Library literature is full of plans for improved charging systems, streamlined ordering and cataloging procedures, and in fact better methods of doing everything which can be done, from the administration of million-volume enterprises to the display of book jackets. It is no unusual thing (indeed it is almost standard practice) for a library association to have the title "As Others See Us" as the theme for its annual meeting. Librarians constantly worry about the opinion which their public, or their board of trustees, or their faculty will have of them.

This driving spirit of collective self-criticism, this constant striving for self-improvement, is not uncommon in the business world, but it is relatively unknown to institutions of higher learning except on the football field. Few departments of instruction engage in the critiques of past practice and future endeavor which are commonplace and of almost daily occurrence in libraries. This is mentioned not as an unfriendly criticism of teachers, who probably do a better job by going their ways individually, but to emphasize this outstanding characteristic of the library profession. Librarians always talk shop and never stop talking about library affairs; they work at their jobs with extraordinary concentration; although life may have beaten some of them into submission, most of them are conscious of a suppressed excitement, a series of challenges, a succession of problems, which keeps them on their toes. Since libraries are quiet places, often with an air of somnolence about them, this may be hard for the layman to believe; but those on the inside know that there is always something exciting happening around a library, even though it may lack the spice to make it a popular movie.

II

In the struggle for survival and self-justification, the librarians have some weapons. No one can publicly be against books, any more than he can be against motherhood, social security, installment buying, or any other beneficial institution of the present day. But some people are opposed to books and feel that it is subversive of librarians to make available to the ordinary man the apparatus for thinking. Such people cannot say so, and they can attack only certain books, basing their objections on grounds of their own definitions of moral and patriotic behavior.[3] Therefore the librarian remains the custodian and purveyor of that respectable commodity, the book, and his place in society is secure.

It worries him, however that people do not read enough books, and he does not wait for people to come to him. In universities, of course, the librarian has a captive audience, sent to him by the assignments of the faculty; also he has another and more mature clientele who need no advertising to inform them of the beauties of research. But with the general public the case is different, and the modern public librarian is appalled by the competition to reading set up by radio, television, motion picture, and comic book. However innocuous or even excellent these media may be, they do offer serious competition to the art and recreation of reading. The librarian therefore arranges displays, contests, bookweeks and all sorts of devices to bring the customers in, and he is likely to venture out in a bookmobile to spread the gospel.

"A college training is an excellent thing," said James Russell Lowell, "but, after all, the better part of every man's education is that which he gives himself, and it is for this that a good library should furnish the opportunity and the means." Not content with a merely passive role, the American Library Association has long had its Office for Adult Education and its Adult Services Division, their work designed to help adults continue their educational development and their recreational reading in all types of libraries. The details are not so important as is the rejection of the storehouse idea and the doing of work which lazier and less dedicated people would leave undone.

To the same end, the ALA has promoted the American Heritage Project, to help citizens appreciate their country, and in addition many libraries serve as hosts to the sessions of the Great Books discussion groups. All in all, librarians have a stubborn belief in education, self-given or not, and in the eventual prevalence of truth in any free market of ideas.

III

For all their concern with extracurricular activities, there are times when librarians turn their attention inward to their own libraries. But even in so doing they are conscious of obligations to their readers. The keynote speech for this aspect of the librarian's profession was delivered by James Russell Lowell at the opening of the Free Public Library in Chelsea, Massachusetts, on December 22, 1885. On that occasion he said:

> Formerly the duty of a librarian was considered too much that of a watchdog, to keep people as much as possible away from the books, and to hand these over to his successor as little worn by use as he could. Librarians now, it is pleasant to see, have a different notion of their

trust, and are in the habit of preparing, for the direction of the inexperienced, lists of such books as they think best worth reading.

Bibliographical and reference work has grown much since 1885, but it is to be hoped that the spirit is the same. The application of science to industry has been a major factor in this development. Rapid as the establishment of special libraries by industry has been, an increasing task of reference work has been assumed by the public libraries, and by college libraries beyond the needs of their own teachers and students. The big problem of the present and future is that there is too much potentially useful material. With tens of thousands of articles appearing in thousands of journals, and the number growing every day, it is impossible to find out quickly all that is being done in many fields. Most librarians are concerned about this problem of retrieval of information. It may be that a super-machine will some day give out both references and abstracts in response to a suitable stimulus.

Side by side with reference and circulation are those divisions of the library that go by the name of technical processes. These are the ministrations that go into the preparation of a book, from its ordering to its launching as a fully recorded, labelled, and identified book, ready for circulation. The various methods of acquisition come under technical processes, as also does a considerable amount of record-keeping and, above all, cataloging. Here are the librarians who seldom see the light of day or the public whom they serve, toiling in little cells and workrooms like cooperative insects, each having some organ, sense, or skill more highly developed than any other. These workers, whose tasks might be thought dull and routine by the uninitiated, are in fact fiercely proud of their calling and not infrequently refer to themselves as a *corps d'élite*. Nowhere in the library is there such pride and so much sensitivity. Cataloging can be learned, but the aptitude for it must be hereditary.

"Tell me," said the lady next door, "do all your books have numbers?" They do indeed have numbers, and the principle behind the numbers is to bring order out of potential confusion and to provide a government of laws and not of men. Most librarians know they are mortal, and they seek, in this as in other procedures, to adopt a system which will hold up after they and their personal knowledge have passed from the scene. Few of the frequenters of a library will object to a numbering system of some sort, but the specific assignment of a call number is sometimes open to argument.

Those few libraries which operate with completely closed stacks have no need of a system other than the assignment of a number from one to infinity. Each acquisition can be given a simple accession number and placed in the next vacant spot on the shelves. Books may be designated as small, medium, and large, and arranged by size, which permits much tighter shelving and saves space. But in such a library, where works on ornithology may rest companionably with those on gasoline engines, the delights of browsing cannot be enjoyed; no one can range along the ranges, seeing what the library has on Napoleon or reptilia or astrophysics. Since this practice is not only delightful but almost a necessity for the serious student, it follows that the books on a given subject are kept together in most libraries, at least so far as possible. Sometimes this is not possible, and then sensibilities are wounded. One research man was grieved to find a work on the hymenoptera of North America among works on agricultural statistics. "Are the ants and bees *compelled* to be in such company?" he inquired; "it seems unjust." And plaintively he added, "I love ants and bees." Here is the librarian in a dilemma, torn between his desire to serve his client and the stern rules which dictate that ants and bees, to say nothing of birds, must find themselves now in a section of pure science, now among works on plants and animals considered for the use of man, and again in economics, as in the case of the work just mentioned. Presumably one man's songbird is another man's potpie, and each will want the birdbooks similarly differentiated.

A great deal of trouble is also caused by monographic works in series, where the series element is relatively unimportant. The series is made up, say, of separate works on organic, analytic, and other subdivisions of chemistry; shall they be kept together as a set, or dispersed as their subjects indicate? Some will say one thing, some another, and the librarian, caught like a Secretary of State between two quarreling nations neither of whom he can afford to antagonize, is likely to be gored by at least one horn of another dilemma.

To change the metaphor, there is in this stormy sea of argument over classification one sure and strong haven of refuge, the catalog. Here the librarian can rest his case; here the bee-lover will find his pets all in one hive; here the organic chemist will find all the books on his subject grouped under one heading, whatever may be their fate upon the shelves.

"Catalog" in library parlance means "card catalog," spelled without the final "ue" in all libraries save some in New and Old England. Catalogs in book form exist, and many of the largest libraries are seriously considering the adoption of this form. The Library of Congress issues a multivolume catalog, with supplements, in which all its cards are reproduced on a smaller scale by offset printing; this printed catalog is of inestimable value in the identification and ordering of books. The saving of space afforded by such a catalog is obvious, and so is the convenience to the user, who can scan a whole page, with many entries, at one time; but the disadvantage of issuing a reference book which will necessarily be out of date before it is published is equally obvious.

Now to bear them to the rock of the catalog, the reader and the librarian have one unfailing raft, and this is the Library of Congress card. In 1800, an Act of Congress established a library for the use of the legislators, and this has grown into the world's largest and one of the world's greatest libraries. It is far more than a place for the preparation of speeches which are franked out all over the country; it is more even than a great research institution and a truly national library; it is also the headquarters for a vast bibliographic enterprise, selling printed cards by the millions annually to libraries large and small.

Cards are made and printed for practically all the books cataloged at the Library of Congress, and the fee is modest considering the service rendered. When one orders a book from a dealer, it is customary to order the LC cards from Washington at the same time. These cards come in little packets of three or four or six or whatever number is requisite. They are all duplicates of each other, the necessary distinctive touches being supplied by the recipient. All have the name of the author or other main entry, the title, and much other information about the book. At the bottom of most cards are the LC and the Dewey call numbers, which have been assigned to the book by the subject specialists at the Library of Congress. Whichever system a library uses, the card will serve equally well when the number is copied onto its usual place in the upper lefthand corner. If the library has its own system, as do the Widener at Harvard and the Newberry at Chicago, the same cards may be used; but in such cases a cataloger must assign a number to each book, making sure that it duplicates no other in the library.

Vast as it is, the Library of Congress does not possess all books, particularly older books, and foreign. In such cases, of which there are many, it is necessary to do the work oneself. All the necessary information must be provided, which is called descriptive cataloging, a logical call number assigned, which is called classification, and subject-headings made, which is called subject cataloging. These cardless items are at once the joy and the despair of the cataloger's life. They are necessarily a bit out of the ordinary, and if they were written in Latin a couple of centuries ago, by an author with a fondness for pseudonyms, they present certain problems in accurate classification and description.

Once a given work has been classified, that is to say assigned to its proper branch and twig on the tree of knowledge, and the cards completed, the cards are placed in various strategic locations in the catalog, each serving to locate the book from a different point of view. As Mr. Lowell put it in 1885:

> Cataloging has also, thanks in great measure to American librarians, become a science, and catalogues, ceasing to be labyrinths without a clue, are furnished with fingerposts at every turn. Subject catalogues again save the

beginner a vast deal of time and trouble by supplying
him for nothing with one at least of the results of
thorough scholarship, the knowing where to look for
what he wants.

It comes as a surprise when one first realizes that libraries have more than one card per book, but of course it is
the added entry cards, those in addition to the main or
author card, which makes the catalog of any good library a
magnificent index and series of bibliographies all in one. Librarians do their best to anticipate all wishes and satisfy all
tastes, but they cannot foresee everything and they have difficulty providing that subject-heading which some readers
seem to want, namely "All the Books in Which I Take a
Particular Interest."

An increasing amount of library effort is being spent on
works issued in some kind of series form, generally amount-
ing now to more than 50%. "Serials" is the library term for
all works which are issued periodically or in a series, whether
one is speaking of the daily paper or of the annual volume of
a learned society. In the larger libraries there are both serials
and periodicals departments, but serials is the handy word,
and some libraries have a separate catalog for these works. In
a typical serials catalog are found the title and call number of
each item, a notation if it is currently received, and one or
more holdings cards, on which the volumes actually in the library's possession are ticked off by number or year. In addition another main entry or title card appears in the main catalog. Nothing would appear simpler than to provide this information, particularly if the Library of Congress has made
the basic cards, but there are many pitfalls for the unwary,
and serials cataloging is about as highly specialized an art as
the library can show.

Serials have a way of changing their names and even
their size without warning, providing problems for both cataloger and binder. In addition, publishers of a periodical have
been known to forget where they were and to publish two
successive volumes with the same number; they have also
been known to grow tired and erratic and publish now ten,

now thirteen, numbers of a journal which is supposed to be monthly throughout the year. All this must be duly confirmed and the necessary adjustments made. The changing of titles is the most annoying habit, both for cataloger and reader. Sometimes a journal devoted to several branches of a science will undergo fission, producing several individuals where only one grew before; sometimes the process is fusion, with alliances produced by affection or necessity. Here is a true case history, admittedly extreme, so well described by Erhard Sanders in a periodical called *Serial Slants* (V, 4) that it would be a pity to spoil it by paraphrase:

THE METAMORPHOSES OF A JOURNAL

Once upon a time there lived a little magazine called *Television Engineering*. It was a slender little thing full of useful information and beloved by many.

But along came a big bully with the pompous name of *FM Magazine* and *FM Radioelectronics* which had at one time been infected with the TV virus and thereafter called itself *FM-TV and Radio Communication*. Under this disguise, it devoured little *Television Engineering* and ruminated it from May 1952 till December 1953. After the last big gulp, it became diet-conscious and started the new 1954 quite slender, this time under the moniker of *Communication Engineering*.

But all the previous dissipation now showed its effect and after one brief issue it became so weak that it fell easy prey to another glutton, *Radio-Electronic Engineering*. This character had had quite a career itself. It had entered the world as a sort of appendix to *Radio and Television News* distinguished by a head band with the inscription *Radio-Electronic Engineering Edition of Radio and Television News*. Later it had made itself somewhat more independent and gone as *Radio-Electronic Engineering Section* and then finally eliminated the section.

It can still be seen on the periodicals shelves as *Radio-Electronic Engineering,* but for how long?

Now all these changes of title must be noted by any library possessing this extraordinary piece of bibliographic confusion. Someone is sure to want the journal by one of its earlier names, and therefore a card must be provided for each name, with the notation that one should now look for the holdings under the latest name. If the name is changed again, which has actually happened in the case described by Mr. Sanders, all these cards must be pulled out and changed. Another way, of course, would be to treat each title as a separate serial; but this also involves a lot of careful checking, a multiplication of cards, and complaints by those who want a whole run, whatever its titular vicissitudes.

IV

It is a paradox that librarians suffer on the one hand from public ignorance of their techniques, and on the other from over-familiarity. After all, everyone if he really tries can recite the alphabet and count to a thousand by ones. Therefore everyone feels that he could be a librarian if he had to do it, and devise efficient procedures too, probably simpler than those generally in use. History teachers, for example, suffer from the same handicap of their craft's not being sufficiently mysterious, whereas no one thinks that he can give advice to mathematicians and physicists, for their knowledge is much too abstruse.

The librarian is torn between his inclination to make his profession appear as a science and his hope that the public will try to understand the rules, which are simple enough though rather numerous. When on his professional dignity his reactions may be likened to the time when King James the First, in one of his many skirmishes with the Common Law and its defender, Chief Justice Sir Edward Coke, said that since law was based on reason, and since the royal reason was acknowledged to be superior to all others, therefore he could judge all cases himself. To this Sir Edward replied that the law was indeed based upon reason, but that it was not natural reason but artificial reason, which took years of study and experience to acquire. So with the librarian. And although the librarian has a good territory and a good product to sell, he cannot always retreat into the mysteries of his craft and ask his public and his Board to support him on faith alone. Faith will take him up to a point, but beyond that he must achieve his effects by statistics of work performed, cost-accounting of at least a rudimentary sort, and reasonable explanations of why his procedures are necessary and not merely boondoggling.

Just as a teacher, in a momentary fit of depression, will think that a university would be a nice place if there were no students, so a librarian will occasionally reflect that his job would be a pleasant one if no one gave him any books. This is because he knows how much it costs to put a book through the mill and maintain it on his shelves. Those who cheerfully say "these books won't cost you anything" have not followed through. A recent survey made by the distinguished Librarian Emeritus of Harvard, Dr. Keyes Metcalf, calculates that each gift book costs his institution $5.75.[4] This sum may be subdivided as follows: purchase price, acquisition costs, and binding are nil, although if the book is unlucky or over-popular it may have to be rebound some day. Incidentally, Dr. Metcalf estimates that the cost of the needed rebinding, relabelling, and repair of material already in his stacks would come to $265,000; but his library is larger than most. To continue: 25 cents is estimated as the cost of checking in and handling the gift book, and $3 as the cost of cataloging. These costs include materials used but mainly refer to the salaries of the staff members concerned. The construction cost of the space occupied by the book is estimated as $1.50, and the endowment required to provide future income for maintenance is $1. This last would include shelving, dusting, issuing, reshelving, and so on. All this adds up to $5.75 Even if the item of $1.50 for construction cost of the space occupied is rejected as being rather arbitrarily introduced, the cost would still be $4.25, which many would consider a very conservative estimate.

If the book is purchased, not only must the purchase price be added, but also the much higher costs for ordering, so that a $3 book works out to $10. With a periodical, the cost is higher yet, for binding must be added. This is said not to discourage people from giving books to libraries, but to emphasize a sometimes overlooked but obviously fundamental part of library operations. Some of the best things in life are free, but not books.

Having acquired his book, the librarian cannot always forget it. He may, for one reason or another, have trouble keeping it. A question endemic in all university libraries is whether or not to centralize. If all the books are kept in one building, some of the scholars will wish that their particular books could be housed in a departmental library. This is particularly true of those scholars who sit up all night with projects and experiments, like the architects and many of the scientists, and want to have their books at their elbows. The librarian, reverting to the setting-hen psychology of the 19th century, hates to see this happen, and he has his reasons too. He knows that a dispersion of the books will greatly weaken his collection, for example that the removal of works on physics from the proximity of works on mathematics will mean that these two related disciplines will not continue to strengthen each other; he also knows that the chances of loss and damage are greatly increased when books leave the central roof; and he knows that even under the best supervision, which is seldom forthcoming in departmental libraries, there is grave danger of uncoordinated policies and unnecessary duplication.

The Metcalf Report shows that while the space problem alone forced Harvard to decentralize, to say nothing of the widely separated locations of some of Harvard's colleges and departments, the results have not been entirely happy; aside from other difficulties just mentioned, hardly any two libraries in that great system follow the same cataloging code, and the results are disastrous for the efficient maintenance of a central or union catalog. At another university some years ago, the autonomy of the departmental libraries was so complete and so wilfully exercised that it took a truly heroic reform to bring order out of a chaotic situation. At another, the librarians of the branches like law and medicine are not appointed by the President upon recommendation of the

Director of Libraries, but rather upon that of the Deans; doubtless this plan works well at the moment, but it could promote disharmony. Therefore the typical university librarian has taken a Hippocratic oath never to permit decentralization to occur; if lack of space or other considerations have forced him to farm his books out, he hopes that the rustlers will not change the brands.

Similarly the librarian is bound by the rules of his order to resist the kindly-meant importunities of those who seek to donate special collections. A special collection is a group of books which is arbitrarily kept in a certain room or on a certain shelf in a library, regardless of the positions which the books would normally occupy. If all special collections were large and unique gatherings of valuable material on a single subject, there would be few problems other than the ever-present one of finding the space somewhere, but many offerings are not of this type. Rather they represent the work of a collector whose tastes were catholic, ranging from architecture to zoology; these books the librarian is expected to keep inviolate and unseparated, out of respect to the individual's feelings or to his memory. Many librarians think that if they could have inscribed upon their tombstones the legend "He Never Accepted a Special Collection" they would have done enough to win the gratitude of posterity, for this turning of a library into a museum of fixed memorials has little to commend it. It is costly all along the line, in cataloging, in shelving, and in management, and it is timewasting for readers who want to find their books readily.

For more desirable material, all libraries, even the richest, face the problem of book selection. Obviously the first determinant will be the function which the library is supposed to discharge. A special library of an oil company will have one task, a junior college library another, and so on. In the case of a public library the problem is especially difficult, for it is hard to tell how far to go in acquiring material for true research purposes, such items being comparatively rare, costly, and little used once they are acquired. In colleges, where faculty recommendation is the most important factor in book selection, the policy is usually that of "building to strength" or to obvious faculty interest where strength does not yet exist.

The modern trend, which should ease this problem of there being more useful books and serials than money with which to buy and process them, goes by the name of cooperative acquisition. This has many variations, but the gist of it is that one library will buy one thing, another library another, and that they will share. There is already a brisk business throughout the country in interlibrary loans, but the new plans will make this more equitable.

An important development on a national scale is the Farmington Plan (named for the town where the agreement was made), by which a large number of important libraries, both academic and public, have agreed that each will be responsible for all procurable library materials on one or more fields or countries. Thus one will take music, another Dutch and Flemish literature, another the Union of South Africa, and so on. The intent is to make sure that at least everything current is received in at least one United States library, but there are also possible economies in this division of labor, and the plan should be a benefit to scholars.

Another well-established project, which will be imitated in other parts of the country, is the Midwest Inter-library Center, in Chicago. This is a large warehouse where the least-used material of a number of large mid-western university libraries is kept, thus easing their space problems. Any of this material can be made available to the owner or to the other partners in a very short time, for it is cataloged and adequately supervised. In addition the participants have reached an agreement whereby each shall be responsible for subscribing to certain serials and periodicals, mainly in foreign languages, for which there is comparatively little demand; no one library therefore has to buy everything.

Union catalogs, as for example the one kept at Emory of the holdings of the Atlanta libraries and of the University of Georgia, are becoming more common, and their value is obvious. In Chicago, it has been agreed that the Newberry Library shall devote itself to the Humanities, the John Crerar Library to Science and Technology, and the Art Institute to the Fine Arts, thus relieving the Public Library of the research materials problem and allowing it to concentrate on general reference, current fiction and standard classics, children's books, and do-it-yourself manuals. Sometimes cooperation can be less formal: for example it would be wasteful for a college in a city where there are already large libraries devoted to law and medicine to spend much in these fields; on the other hand its collections in political science and biology may be of great value to lawyers and doctors who qualify as borrowers because of their research interests. This kind of cooperative acquisition does not require an agreement, but merely common sense.

So, presented in a few snapshots, we have our librarian. Whatever his function in the library, he or she is a good deal more than a label-pasting, book-mending drudge. He has with some consistency stood for democratic principles and intellectual freedom. He believes in books, although he has little time to read them himself. He has a lot of rules and procedures which he at least believes are necessary to provide good service. It may take time, but if you will leave your name and address, he will get you the book.   □

[1] Helen E. Haines, "Ethics of Librarianship," *Library Journal,* LXXI (15 June 1946), 848-851.

[2] The writer is well aware that few women make it to the top in university libraries, but the American Library Association has had many women presidents, and in general there is equality of opportunity.

[3] The librarians' answer, expressing the convictions of the vast majority of the profession, was contained in the statement "The Freedom to Read," published among other places in the Summer, 1953, issue of the *AAUP Bulletin.* This official statement of the ALA affirms the duty of the librarian to make available material showing "the widest diversity of views and expressions," not to intrude his own opinions, not to label books in other than the literal sense, and to resist encroachments upon the people's freedom to read.

[4] *Report on the Harvard University Library; a Study of Present and Prospective Problems* (Cambridge, Mass., 1955).

THIS LIBRARIAN'S CREDO

Charlotte Georgi

When I read the library literature about what a library is and
what a librarian should be—long lists of lofty aims and worthy, if abstruse, objectives, usually fully expounded in a
plethora of sesquipedalian terms—I am duly impressed but a
bit wearied.

Therefore, I began to think about what I believe about
my profession after some years of experience (too many to
be more specific) as a middle-management librarian (and
probably bragging at that). I even hope, vainly enough, that
my words may come to the attention of some younger librarians and may give them courage, or guidance, or maybe just a
great big laugh.

So, just what do *I* believe as a practicing librarian who is
a part-time administrator, part-time supervisor, part-time
"Dear Abby," part-time public relations department, part-
time personnel manager, part-time budget director, part-time
paper-pusher, part-time fund raiser, part-time rare books expert, part-time janitor, too-little-time reference-bibliographer-
teacher-author-lecturer, and full-time griper?

Like the seven virtues, or, better still, the seven vices, I
have seven tenets of belief I have classified (as any good librarian would) as follows: 1) Dignity, 2) Virtue, 3) Sex,

Reprinted with permission of author and publisher from *Special
Libraries*, 57 (no. 5): p. 305-307, May-June, 1966. Copyright © by
Special Libraries Association.

4) Communications, 5) Simplification, 6) Automation, and 7) Books.

CREDO I: DIGNITY

I believe in the dignity of the librarian as a Librarian—not that he who can does, he who can't teaches, and he who really can't do anything becomes a librarian. I believe that librarians are made, not born, although the latter definitely helps.

I believe that the librarian must act, appear, and be worthy of respect—in a word (or several), that he should respect himself and his work and not confuse his backbone with a wet dishrag.

I become sick of the endless discussions of "The Image of the Librarian" and "Is Librarianship a Profession?", except for the excellent essay of Henry Madden in the July 1964 *California Librarian* and Eric Moon's rejoinder in the February 1, 1965, *Lj.*

I don't believe that librarians necessarily have to have a vocation and hear voices, although after a while most of them probably do. I do not go so far as to say we need to be burned at the stake. (Listening to most of the talks at library conventions is quite enough.) But, I also don't believe that the meek will inherit the earth or that sweet little old maid librarians will ever get very far.

I believe in asking and expecting of others only as much as I demand of myself. I believe in setting a good example, but I have given up looking for carbon copies of perfect ME.

I believe in the near-divinity of the creative imagination, whether applied to crafty maneuvering for a convenient parking space assignment, devising a better method of processing overdue notices, or making the maximum most out of the minimum of library staff, time, space, budget, or whatever.

I believe in WORK being a *raison d'etre,* not something to be chatted through from 8 a.m. to 5 p.m. I believe that one's work should be re-creation, in the creative sense of the word. Work SHOULD be fun. If it isn't, find something else to do. In other words, I believe in a 168 hour week.

CREDO II: VIRTUE

I believe in virtue, in general, but, then again, vice has its
virtues. Virtue in excess can always become a vice. I MUST
remind myself of this!

I believe that order, organization, efficiency, and economy in every respect are essential to a good library operation.
I especially believe that punctuality is the courtesy of
princes[1] and, like cleanliness, is next to godliness, perhaps
even nexter. While I am at it, I like courtesy, too.

I believe that any decision is better than no decision, although it is granted that no decision at all is really a form of
decision. I do not believe in administration by committee and
group-thinking. I do not believe in the Thomas Nast-Boss
Tweed Ring cartoon showing the ring of ward politicians
pointing their fingers at each other in consecutive circular
order passing on the blame. I do believe in the sign on Harry
Truman's presidential desk, *The Buck Stops Here.*

I still have to think about honesty being the best policy,
especially if you'll probably be caught anyway. This is a
virtue to which the great American library public obviously
gives only lip service, as witness the shocking reports of
"lost" book statistics.

I believe one should put up and shut up or get out. In
other words, I believe in loyalty. If you can't respect the
people you work with and for, if you are chronically dis-
satisfied, GET OUT. The world is a wide and wonderful
place, full of opportunities for anyone who can read and
write, admittedly rather rare and special skills these illiterate
days. Of course, at some time one must settle down, especially as one becomes older. In that case, shut up. This is probably a good idea for older people anyway (Am I a case in
point?); it's also good for younger people, young people, old
people, and children.

CREDO III: SEX

I believe in sex—that men are men and women are women,
even if librarians. I know that women are inferior and accept
it as an asset. I never carry a thumbtack if a man is around. If

I am inferior, I want to be treated with all of the courtesy due an inferior. Incidentally, I know that even if we can't beat 'em, we can outlive 'em. Fortunately, I spend most of my working day surrounded by the handsome men of the UCLA Graduate School of Business Administration—and I love it!

Quite seriously, what I am trying to say to the young ladies is this—the library world ought not be a feminist forum. Forget the feminine mystique fuss. Do your job. Accept your responsibilities. Don't expect to be treated like a man and excused like a woman.

CREDO IV: COMMUNICATIONS
I believe in communication, in communicating with everyone, even library users, constantly, incessantly, all the time —by news bulletins, slingers, signs, handouts, newsletters, memoranda, even by word of mouth. I loathe writing reports but to write excellent quarterly and annual reports is one of the librarian's essential duties.

I believe in going through one's mail daily, sorting it into file baskets labelled UP (where divine guidance is sought), OUT (for action), and DOWN (into the round file, where most of it so richly belongs). I believe in meeting deadlines punctually—except for quarterly and annual reports.

I believe that a sense of humor never hurt anyone. In fact, humor is better than survival biscuits for a librarian. Solemnity is no guarantee of profundity. It has been my observation that about all that solemnity absolutely guarantees is solemnity.

I believe there is too much chatter and too much of it is frozen into publication. To lift an idea from Clarence Day, I believe in SILENCE, especially in printed form.

I believe that every librarian owes it to his profession, if indeed librarianship is to be respected as a profession, to have a professional hobby such as writing articles and books (inconsistency[2] obviously doesn't bother me, see above paragraph), preparing useful printed materials for other librarians and for library patrons, maintaining active membership in professional organizations, preparing exhibits, or whatever.

CREDO V: SIMPLIFICATION

I believe in simplification, simplification, simplification. Just because something has been done a particular way for the past two centuries doesn't necessarily make it right for 1966, 1976, 1986. I believe in change, not just for the sake of change, but only after careful examination of the case at hand in view of what is actually needed and wanted. This is particularly true of routine procedures. Are all of those little records and cards, much less the information on them, REALLY necessary?

We all suffer from lack of time, space, and staff. The answer, in too many cases, is not more money to buy more time, space, and staff, but more efficient management of these costly resources. Do what you do well—and cut out the nonessentials. You'd be surprised how much you can do without. Of course, this is no way to empire build.

I believe what is best for the library and its staff is inevitably best for the library user, not vice versa (illustrations supplied on request).

I believe red tape should be cut into infinitesimal pieces and stuffed by force down the throats of those who manufacture it.

CREDO VI: AUTOMATION

I believe in computerization of library routines but advocate that a special breed of technicians be created called something else besides librarian—systems analysts, information managers, data processors, or whatever. These are NOT librarians, who by very derivation from the Latin term, *liber,* are concerned with BOOKS. I am all for these technicians and machine experts, but their coats-of-arms should be oil cans rampant on a field of screwdrivers gules.

Incidentally, I am all for book catalogs. UCLA has one (G. K. Hall, 1963), and it is a wonderful time-saver, both for the library staff and for the library user. I can't wait for the computer revolution to reach my library to free me from dull routine work for the things I really want to do—or so the ads say.

Meanwhile, until the much vaunted computer millennium arrives,[3] and it seems to be mightly slow in doing so in libraries, I believe in careful examination and evaluation of existing work procedures and simplification thereof.

CREDO VII: BOOKS
I believe in BOOKS. Larry Powell, add me to your baggage.

CONCLUSION
This is what I believe, not necessarily what I practice. . . . ☐

[1] As Louis XVIII always said, *"L'exactitude est la politesse des rois."*

[2] As Ralph Waldo says, "A foolish consistency is the hobgoblin of little minds. . . ." And I believe in thinking BIG.

[3] It is the author's understanding that a computer has now been constructed that is so human it blames other computers for its mistakes.

DON'T GIVE US YOUR TIRED, YOUR POOR

Margaret Bennett

About a year ago one of our library patrons who was teaching
fourth grade, studying for his supervisory credential, and
moonlighting as an encyclopedia salesman had, as the euphe-
mism goes, a nervous breakdown. He wound up in a state
mental hospital for several months. When he emerged, naturally he was still in a somewhat shattered condition, and the
outpatient counselor at the mental institution started nudging
him toward the ancient and honorable profession of librarianship. "Maybe in a junior or senior high school, because you
already have a teaching credential" were the exact words of
the counselor. On top of that, everyone who knew Jim kept
dropping in to the library and urging us to help "the poor
guy" gain admittance to graduate library school. "It would
be good for him," they said, and obviously he couldn't return
to teaching because "the classroom would be too much of
a strain."

All of this brought home to us the fact that there is an
idea rampant among counselors, educators, and laymen that
the library profession is some sort of great, warm, book-lined
womb into which people who have been knocked about in
life can retreat to spin out their days idly leafing the classics
and saying *"shhhhhhh."*

Reprinted with permission of the authors and the publisher from *The
Atlantic Monthly*, 215: 93-95, May 1965. Copyright © 1965, by The
Atlantic Monthly Company, Boston, Massachusetts.

In the public mind, librarianship seems to have become a kind of American Foreign Legion, the officially recommended "way out" for doctoral candidates who can't screw their courage to the sticking place to take their prelims, for battered teachers who want to escape the classroom, for people in business who buckle under the stress of competition, and for all those college graduates who have never quite figured out what to do with themselves.

One indication of the currency of this belief is that the New York Life Insurance Company in its career booklet "Should You Be a Librarian?" finds it necessary to point out that "librarians are normal human beings" — a bit of information they don't feel compelled to pass on in their booklets about any other profession.

Not only is library service considered a haven for people with emotional and personality difficulties, but just let some aspect of a person's respiratory, digestive, or motor system start acting up to the extent that it affects his work, and see how quickly his family doctor or a concerned friend will spring forward with "You'll have to go into something less demanding, get a job where you can take it easy — Say, I know. You could be a *librarian!*"

Even more alarming to us in librarianship, though, is the other side of this base-metal coin. The same well-meaning citizens who steer the disturbed and sickly *into* our ranks also steer the talented and the vigorous young people whom we so desperately need *away* from library service. Should an athletic, good-looking, debate-team captain and National Merit Scholarship winner make it known that he very sincerely wants to become a librarian, he could expect somewhat the same reaction as the one when a young man announces on the Mike Nichols-Elaine May recording that he has a burning desire to become a registered nurse.

An outstanding girl might get a more indulgent response, for after all, "librarianship *is* a woman's profession." But, still, if she is attractive, everyone will have a "this, too, shall pass" attitude, knowing she will change her mind quickly when Mr. Right comes along.

No, the young people whom our educational institutions propel toward a library career are too often the shy under-achievers who test high in verbal skills and low in math-science, the kind who "read a lot," which frequently means that they sit alone staring at an open book because they have no friends.

Aware that such recruits will have difficulty facing the tremendous challenges of the next decades, library schools are starting to screen their applicants more carefully, refusing to play the role of the midnight mission of the professional schools. As Dr. Martha Boaz, dean of the School of Library Science at the University of Southern California, says, "We're looking for candidates with plenty of physical, mental, and moral muscle. The job of the librarian is becoming increasingly complex and difficult — and library school faculties are determined that the meek shall not, by default, inherit the berth."

Those of us who are already in the field, facing the dual explosions of population and knowledge, agree with Dr. Boaz. Librarianship today *is* very demanding, and we feel it should be so advertised.

Physically, librarians have to be in top shape to face long, exhausting, and, contrary to the myth, nonsedentary days, with evening and weekend assignments often thrown in. Besides that, we need special reserves of energy for chasing the fleet-footed exhibitionist from the stacks and for acting as bouncer when the reading room degenerates into a "teen-age nightclub."

When Deborah King, the former head of the UCLA library circulation department, was asked to name the most important quality in a candidate for a library job, her immediate reply was "Good feet!" Now, while this misses a few of the qualities we feel are indispensable for most professional library positions, it comes closer to what we really need than what the public thinks.

Intellectually, no profession demands a greater breadth of knowledge from its members. The entire world's fund of information — now doubling in size every year — is our realm, and we must be able to call forth the most obscure fact rapidly and accurately, often with disaster simmering in the background. Recently, for example, in a Gulf coast town a volatile chemical broke loose from its container and flared up, threatening to destroy the dock area. The fire department put in an emergency call to the public library in order to find out the properties of the escaping liquid. With the infromation supplied by the library the fire was quickly brought under control.

In a large urban area, such as Los Angeles, the library reference desks give out more than ten million answers a year, answers that not only help keep docks from burning, but bridges from collapsing, businesses from failing, and human beings from disintegrating.

A good librarian, however, does not confine himself to the prevention of disaster. Just as often he may find himself playing the role of midwife to a miracle. As Catherine Drinker Bowen said, "A scholarly librarian stands at times in the relation of editor. By tactful approach the librarian will discover the scheme of one's book, how widely one plans to explore. . . . What he says can encourage expansion, a deeper treatment."

But if we librarians had to choose the most vital fiber in our professional makeup, it would be the "moral muscle," that tissue toughened by making difficult decisions and sticking by them. One such decision was made on that November, 1963, weekend by Jerome Cushman, head of the New Orleans Public Library. He had to decide quickly whether or not to release to the press the titles of the library books read by Lee Harvey Oswald. Cushman explains his action in these words: "I am a strong advocate of the civil right of privacy, and I consider a patron's reading habits as inviolable as the secrets of the confessional, but I decided that this information should be released to help block the hysterical rumors and inflammatory accusations already starting to fly in all directions."

Of course, not all librarians' decisions achieve the

national prominence of Mr. Cushman's, but every day librarians are taking stands that vitally affect the life of our democracy. Some are as deceptively simple as that of the librarian in a Southern state who, in defiance of a posted, ill-defined local ordinance and without consulting his library board, waged a quiet and bloodless war of attrition against the "colored" and "white" signs over the drinking fountains, patiently taking them down and putting them up again until finally he could leave them down for good.

Then there is always the day-to-day battle of the book collection. Every pressure group in the community believes it has an inalienable right to use the library as its own personal propaganda distribution center and a concomitant right to censor out any materials presenting an opposing viewpoint. The librarian's code of ethics requires that he maintain a book collection representing all points of view. Consequently, he may find himself laying his job on the line in defense of reading matter which is loathsome to him personally. Not long ago a California junior college librarian, a staunch liberal himself, was called before the faculty library committee to justify the library's purchase of the *John Birch Society Blue Book*.

A librarian who tries to supply his community with more than shelves filled with vellum-covered pablum can expect to be simultaneously spattered with such opposing epithets as religious bigot and atheist, fascist and "dirty Commie," bluenosed censor and leering pornographer. When these tags are also pinned on the members of his family, it takes muscle not only of the moral but also of the visceral variety to persevere.

Today, opportunities in the library field are limitless. There is an estimated shortage of 100,000 professional librarians. A talented person can shoot to the top possibly more rapidly here than in any other profession. But that word "talented" should be emphasized. The person who cannot succeed in some other field cannot expect to honor the library profession with his presence and immediately rise to the position of Librarian of Congress. No, if he has the

personal qualities that would make him a low-grade teacher
or social worker or lawyer, the chances are he will be a low-
grade librarian as well, and we have no need for low-grade
librarians.

All of this may sound as if we librarians wanted to slam
the door in the face of anyone with the slightest physical or
emotional difficulty, as if we wanted no one who is not a
brilliant, hardworking, perfectly adjusted, clean, brave, and
reverent Jack Armstrong. This is not true. In the first place, it
would be impossible to find such flawless specimens, and in
the second, all that perfection would make us a deadly dull
group. All we really want is to have people enter into librarianship as they enter into any other profession, not *because*
of their personal handicaps, but *in spite of* them. We want
people to become librarians for positive reasons — because
they have a consuming interest in ideas and knowledge and
because they have strong public-service feelings, rather than
because they happen to have asthma or a cosmetic difficulty
or a hormonal imbalance or a touch of schizophrenia.

If, as President Kennedy believed, "the library is the key
to progress and the advancement of knowledge," then the librarians of the future are destined to carry an immense responsibility. So please don't give us your tired, your poor.
Give us your vigorous, your rich in spirit and intellect, and
the library profession will return their gifts to you a
thousandfold. □

THE PROFESSIONAL ROLE OF THE LIBRARIAN

Lester Asheim

Anyone in this audience who has seen as many as ten moving pictures in his lifetime will undoubtedly have seen at least five in which this familiar plot development occurs. Somewhere along about the fifth reel, the rich young businessman turns to his secretary with amazement and remarks: "I've never seen you without your glasses before, Miss Pomfret. Why—you're beautiful!" The rich, deathless dialogue then probably goes on along these lines: "I think I've never seen the real YOU before. For the first time I'm seeing you, not as a secretary, but as a woman!"

This is such a cliché of film making that even Hollywood pokes fun at it now, but as usual with most of the recurring situations in the popular arts, its continued appeal can be accounted for on these grounds, that—oversimplified and exaggerated though it may be—the situation illustrates a basic fact of human experience. And the audience, whether consciously or subconsciously, recognizes it to be a true one. The truth that is illustrated is this: that we ourselves often raise the barriers which militate against our being seen for what we really are; that the failure of others to appreciate our worth may derive from a failure of our own to bring our worth to their attention.

Reprinted from *2 Library Lectures* (Emporia: Kansas State Teachers College, 1959, pp. 5-13) by permission of the author and the Graduate Program in Librarianship, Kansas State Teachers College, Emporia, Kansas.

164

You will remember that in these Cinderella fantasies, it is the heroine rather than her boss who is really to blame for the delayed response. The more worldly, gum-chewing girl-friend—who is wiser than our heroine, if not so bright—is the one who points out to her that by being efficient, unobtrusive, the perfect secretary, she has made it impossible for anyone to see her as anything else. What is required is that our heroine recognize her own potentialities, and stepping out of the perfect secretary's role for a moment, draw attention to her natural charms and abilities by displaying rather than disguising them. The change that occurs therefore, is not really an exterior one—the removal of the glasses—but an interior one—a reevaluation of herself. The removal of the glasses is symbolic.

This may seem to you to be a pretty far-fetched device for leading into a discussion of the librarian's professional role, but it is not as remote as you may think. There is a tenable parallel here, I think, between Hollywood plot #13-B, and the plight of the average librarian—male or female. For we, like our heroine, deserve a recognition we have not always received, and in our case as in hers, the barrier is largely of our own making.

That barrier is more than a pair of glasses, although glasses make a good symbol for what I am talking about. For the barrier is the way we look at ourselves and at our responsibilities as librarians. It is my contention that like the Hollywood heroine I've been describing we have too long underestimated our own importance. Our responsibilities as librarians are of more significance than we seem to be aware.

If you were to ask every third person you pass on the street during the next few days to give you a one-word description of librarians, I would guess that about 83 per cent of them—in a manner of speaking—would come up with the adjective: "Mousy." Now I maintain that this has nothing to do with the way librarians look. We represent as great a variety of sizes and shapes as any other professional group; there are young librarians and old ones; males and females; short and tall; handsome and not so handsome. But "mousy"

connotes a kind of nondescriptness—a kind of invisibility—
which effectively hides how we look beneath an impenetrable
cloak of self-effacement and deprecation. As Chesterton has
pointed out in one of his Father Brown stories, the really invisible man is someone who is so completely accepted as part
of the landscape that we have stopped seeing him. (In this
particular story, although all of the witnesses have seen the
murderer come and go into an apartment house in broad day-
light, not one recalls him. The reason is that he wore the
uniform of a postman, and a postman is so much a part of the
natural scene that he becomes, for all practical purposes, invisible because unremarkable.) The librarian is in much the
same case: we are considered mousy because we tend to disappear into the woodwork. We are only half seen and heard
because no one stops to look at us or listen; we are merely
unremarkably and unobtrusively there.

The fault is ours; we scuffle out of the way of recognition. We tend to think of ourselves as "only" librarians, as
though half ashamed of our effrontery in occupying space at
all. When we are asked our occupation, our reply is half apology if not downright evasion. Until we remove that kind of
glasses, no one is ever going to look at us and say, "Why,
you're beautiful"—or important—or useful—or indeed, even a
human being.

And yet the librarian is somebody—somebody rather
important in his community and in society. He has responsibilities as serious and as influential in their social effects as
those of the professor, the banker, the lawyer, or the senator.
But before society can recognize this we must recognize it
ourselves. So today I am going to take time out to tell you
something you ought to know already but apparently do not:
I am going to tell you how important you are.

Let us look first at the library, and its place in the community. A library, by definition, is any collection of books—
but THE library, the institution which the professional
schools are preparing their students for, is not just any collection of books. It is a selected collection, organized and
administered to serve certain specific social ends. The library

is a social agency, it is an agency of communication, an agency for education. It is different from, and considerably more than, the collection of books represented in a book store. It is different from, and considerably more than, such a channel as radio, television or film for the dissemination of ideas. It is different from, and if not more than, certainly as important in its differences from, the school and the college as an educational institution.

The functions it serves in our society are vital to the achievement of the best aims of that society. No other agency achieves quite so well the informal, "client-centered" (if I may borrow that barbarous term from the counselors) kind of self-education which a democratic people needs to exist in today's world. No other agency provides the variety of entertainment, education and information that will meet the needs and interests of almost any audience rather than those of a pre-determined audience, defined by its size and its willingness to pay for services rendered in the consumption of goods. No other agency provides under a single roof, preservation of the heritage of the past, a flexible reflection of the major currents of the present, and the planned preparation for needs and interests of the future.

The persons who are responsible for the establishment, organization, efficient functioning and continuing growth of such an agency are obviously people of importance in the community. If they are to achieve these ends, they must take real leadership: in the selection of materials, in the creation of services, in the identification of needs. They are, in the very best sense of the word, professional people: dedicated to high standards of performance, relying upon the application of principles and the use of judgment, and devoted to a code of ethical practice concerned, not with self-interest, but with service to others.

Now I submit that anyone who "only" does these things is doing quite enough, and that "only" should drop from our vocabulary. I'm a librarian—not "only a librarian." And there is plenty of reason to be proud of it, if we live up to our own ideal of what library service should be. That ideal departs considerably from the standard stereotype of the mousy librarian. But oddly enough we are going to have to destroy that stereotype not only in the minds of the public, but even in the minds of librarians themselves, whose self-image is far from flattering.

A good first step could be taken on a fairly obvious and surface level. Because I believe in the power of words and of stereotypes, I should like to suggest that one thing we could do is abandon, right now, the "handmaiden" concept of librarianship. "Handmaiden" connotes subservient response to the initiative of others, and librarians do more than perform a handy and convenient service. They play a dynamic and creative social role. They are not merely the stage hands—they design the set. For it is the librarian who makes it possible for the scholar, the researcher, and the casual reader to make the kind of demands they make with some reasonable assurance that they can be satisfied. It is the librarian who shapes the collection, organizes the services and creates the atmosphere and the machinery that brings those demands into being. Thus he does more than assume the tiresome, grubbing tasks which other busier people do not have the time to assume. He does something that the others, however important in their own field, are not equipped to do, and for which they have a greater need than they know: he makes available one of the few channels through which the free access to the best in the world of ideas is kept open.

This is what underlies everything we do as librarians, although we sometimes become so interested in the process that we forget what the processes are for. When we select some books and reject others; when we assign classification numbers and determine catalog entries; when we experiment with new machines for the retrieval of knowledge and concern ourselves with devices for bibliographical control; when we design new buildings or reorganize our departmental arrangements; when we introduce discussion programs, or film forums, or record concerts, or exhibits—the purpose is always to promote freer, more reliable, and virtually unique access to the wide world of ideas.

Now it seems to me that anyone in a position so demanding, so challenging, of such social importance would want to describe his work to others in terms that would convey some sense of this. And it disturbs me profoundly that, more often than not, librarians do not speak of librarianship in that way, but instead describe it as "oodles of fun" and a great big game. The latest, in a long line of illustrious spokesmen for librarianship to use this approach is Allan Angoff, whose article "The Male Librarian—An Anomaly?" you may have read in the February 15, 1959, *Library Journal.* If I seem to pick on Mr. Angoff it is not because his article is by any stretch the worst of these, but merely because it is the most recent. Mr. Angoff, you will remember, is disturbed by the look of pity, the sad commiseration, the disbelief with which his choice of a library career is greeted by non-librarians. His answer, and I quote, is: "I do not defend library work, I do not keep calling it a profession and I usually avoid that word, but I speak of the excitement I find in my work." He acknowledges that librarianship entails a lot of piddling paper work, but reminds us that ". . . hospitals and universities and atomic laboratories also struggle with lots of paper and they have a multitude of other problems which seem to have nothing to do with medicine, education, and atomic research." What of that?—Mr. Angoff points out that librarianship is fun. "I see our whole society mirrored in the library . . . bewildered retired people, regular down-and-outers . . . ladies who read only best sellers and men who only read mysteries and murder novels. Antique lovers . . . genealogy bugs . . . bridge fanatics . . . inveterate readers of newspaper and magazines . . ." And his clincher is "Even my clergyman friend, sad eyes and all at my plight and pay as a librarian, did grant that I seemed delighted with my work."

All very charming, of course. But if you were to ask a hobo why he chooses to live his kind of life instead of doing something more constructive his answer would probably be something like this: "While you slave and worry in your hospital, or laboratory, or factory, I lie on my back, on the cool grass looking up at the blue sky, and listen to the birds

sing. I have much more fun than you do." We might grant
that he does seem to have more fun, but such a reply seldom
wins our respect. We expect men to have a greater sense of
social responsibility than that, and if the man is one whose
talents would make it possible for him to make a contribution to society, we deplore the waste. Mr. Angoff's defense of
librarianship as a career is essentially the hobo's reply, yet he
professes surprise that his neighbors look at him with sad
eyes.

When Mr. Angoff compares the work of the library with
that of the hospital, the university, and the atomic laboratory, he sees a parallel only in the amount of time-consuming
paper work that goes on in all of them. Had he pushed his
comparison just one more step, he might then have come to
the real key to his problem and maybe even to an understanding of why even he happened to choose the hospital, the university and the atomic laboratory with which to make his
comparison. For the doctor, the educator, the scientist have
status because of the service they render to society. Men who
work at a job worth doing don't bother to defend it because
of the personal pleasure it gives them. It goes without saying
that there will be satisfaction in an occupation that performs
such services.

The librarians' *raison d'être* lies in what we have to give
to others, rather than in what we can selfishly get for ourselves. I do not think that we will win the respect of non-
librarians—or even that we will recruit good young people for
librarianship—if we can say nothing more for our (if you will
excuse the expression) profession than that it is so much fun,
and you meet such interesting people. On these grounds, the
hat check girl at the Stork Club has us beat a hundred ways.
But we have her beat on the importance of the service we
perform—and that's where our defense, it seems to me,
properly lies.

Am I saying, then, that there is no joy in library work—
or that I do not think that librarians ought to get pleasure
from what they do? Of course not. As a matter of fact I
doubt if one could be a librarian if he did not love what he is

doing and want to do it more than any other thing. Well, then, why not call it fun? At this point in my interior dialogue—because I went through a bit of soul searching here to discover why I resisted what seems to be so popular a defense of librarianship—I asked myself, "Would you think it odd if a doctor said it was fun to perform operations; if a judge said he just loves trying cases; if a minister said saving souls is his favorite game?" When I put the question that way I suddenly knew the answer. I certainly would think it odd! And I knew why. Because, in every one of the true professions, the goal is not fun for the professional man but the benefit of those he serves. The doctor, the lawyer, the churchman find satisfaction and fulfillment (not just fun) and they find it in what they can do for others and not in the pursuit of personal pleasure. The real defense of librarianship should be that we perform an essential and unselfish service. When we try to win the respect of our neighbors or when we try to make librarianship attractive to good young people we will have to do more than say that it is fun, for that turns the whole meaning of the profession upside down.

My first paradox leads to a second. Having disposed of the apparent contradiction which exists where I want the librarian to like what he is doing but not do it for fun, I come to a second problem. Because those who think librarianship would be fun are almost invariably those who feel that they are qualified for librarianship because they "just love books." And while I am convinced that the librarian must love books, I look with considerable suspicion on those who consider a love of books alone to be a sufficient qualification.

I'm aware that from this time forward there will be those who accuse me of having said that a librarian need not love books, that books do not matter, etc., etc. I did not, of course, say these things at all. I said—or at least I now say here: the love of books, an interest and delight in them; a knowledge of books and the desire to work with them, are essentials for the good librarian. But they are not in themselves enough. The trouble with those who make a profession of loving books is that they think it *is* enough. And because of this we are faced with the widely held belief that librarianship requires none of the qualifications that any of the other professions require; one need only love books. The love of books is indeed what we build our profession upon; without it there could not be librarianship at all. A librarian who doesn't love books is like a ship captain who is susceptible to sea sickness or a surgeon who faints at the sight of blood. Yet obviously no one would put himself up to be the captain of a ship on the sole grounds that "I don't get sea sick," nor would a candidate for medical school consider himself sufficiently qualified solely because he was able to watch operation without queasiness. These qualifications are taken for granted; but in each case the professional qualifications must be much, much more than that.

As a matter of fact, the "love of books" should also be much more than is implied in the term as it is now used by many librarians. A love of books is taken in some quarters as being, not a devotion to the ideas books carry, but to the artifact itself. A book lover is defined, apparently, not so much as one who reads books, but rather as one who fondles them. The container rather than the thing contained has become a kind of fetish; it becomes a major concern that the book be well printed rather than well written; that it feel good to the hand more than that it say something to the mind or heart. These concerns with the look and feel of the book as an artifact are legitimate enough in their proper place, and that place might well be first for the private collector. But the librarian—and certainly the public librarian—is not a private collector; he is a professional educator. His business is not only with books themselves, but with the underlying values books so abundantly embody. That books that are well designed, well bound and well printed are pleasanter to read may be taken for granted. But our first concern should be that what they have to say is worth reading.

For one of the first requirements of the professional librarian is the ability to select books to serve the needs and interests of readers. Such purposeful selection implies a love of books all right, a knowledge of them, and an understanding of the ways in which they can be used. But it also implies the recognition that the librarian's concern is not with the books because they are books, but with books because they promote the objectives of the library. The library's objectives—to educate, to inform, to entertain, and to inspire—are reached through books, but only when the books are selected, evaluated, interpreted, organized and made available for use. The better these tasks are performed the better the library, and this means that the librarian must do more than read books for his own pleasure. It means that he must do all that he can to demonstrate to his library's potential users the ways in which books can serve and sustain them. This demands of him that he love books and read them, but it also demands of him that he devise the systems, build the buildings, and initiate the services that will bring the book and the reader together and give the book its maximum opportunity to do its work.

So let no one tell you that you have failed librarianship if all you have done is increased your book budget, built new and attractive branches, and worked for the extension of library services, in order to introduce books to someone who never used them before. That, it seems to me, is precisely what the librarian is supposed to do. That is why I have underlined the professional character of librarianship.

Now when I say "professional" I am not referring to the completion of a certain number of courses in a library school, but to an attitude and a point of view towards the work we do. A professional librarian is not necessarily the same thing as a person who works in a library, or even—unfortunately—a person who holds a degree in librarianship. He is someone who knows not only what to do and how to do it, but why he is doing it—and the why has to do with the people we serve. The true librarian is not just a collector of dead books; he is a selector of living ones, and he gives them life for many readers through the tools of his profession. These tools may be as mundane as a shelving arrangement; as crass as a new and attractive building; as far-reaching as a policy of service; as intangible as book knowledge; and as infectious as his enthusiasm. None of these are ends in themselves; all of them are means for making the book more available, more attractive, more exciting to the users, real and potential, of the library.

It is only natural, I suppose, that librarians, in describing the importance of their work, have tended to describe, not librarianship, but the book. Western civilization has, to a very real degree, rested upon the written records of man's achievements and ideas. "The best that is known and thought in the world" has been available to all of us, and almost solely through the book. The particular pleasure that the reader can find in literary style can be duplicated in no other medium. The time needed to think about what is being said is provided in no other medium. The ability to deal with all aspects of the subject, to take as long as the subject requires (and not as long as the sponsor dictates or the length of the newspaper column, or the amount of time that one can comfortably remain seated in a theater) is again almost solely a characteristic of the book. None of the other media of communication, no matter how attractive, or available, or simple to use they may be, can provide us with the exercise of the mind and the judgment, the opportunity for rational analysis and verification, the stimulation of new thoughts and the generation of new ideas, which the book provides. It is not only a resource of existing ideas but a mental discipline which stimulates the creation of new ones, and this, particularly in a period like the present, and in a democracy, is extremely important. These things need to be said, and librarians generally are the ones to say them.

This defines the values of the book; it does not tell us much about librarianship. The important thing for us to add to our comments is the role that the library plays in making this essentail, invaluable, and incomparable instrument available. To get the right book to the right reader at the right time requires special techniques and special talents, and while it may be true that the librarian is important because of the values of books, the values of the book might all too often be lost completely but for the mediation of the librarian.

I am suggesting that librarians should bring this fact to the attention of those whom we do or could serve. That we have not done so before is in no small measure due to the fact that we seem not yet fully to realize it ourselves. The barrier to our deserved recognition is partially of our own making; it lies in our willingness to relinquish important responsibilities to others often less well qualified than ourselves, because of our conviction, or our readiness to accept the evaluation of others, that we are—after all—only librarians. When we erase that "only;" when we step forward proudly and say "Give me these responsibilities; after all I am the librarian!", we will no longer be mousy but men. And then—and only then—can we expect the community to turn to us with gratified surprise to say, "I never really saw you before—without your glasses!"

THE PROFESSIONAL DECISION

Lester Asheim

Yesterday, assured of a really captive audience, I took advantage of the occasion to let off some long-accumulated steam about the librarian's own view of his professional importance. To many of you who were there, it may have seemed that I was guilty, at least of ill-becoming immodesty, if not of downright unscientific exaggeration. My claims about the importance of the librarian to his community and about the professional character of librarianship may have been flattering to voice and to hear, but some of you may have wondered how great the actual distance is between the ideal professional stature I was claiming, and the reality of practice for most librarians. After all, I made things easy for myself by speaking in broad general terms of the aims and objectives of librarianship as I see them. If I were to look a little more intensively at what librarians accomplish instead of what they profess, would we still look so good?

For those of you who were not in yesterday's audience, let me say merely that I called for stronger conviction on the part of librarians themselves that we are engaged in a truly professional activity dedicated to the performance of an essential and unselfish service to others; that this service is of sufficient social value for us to acknowledge it with pride

Reprinted from *2 Library Lectures* (Emporia: Kansas State Teacher College, 1959, pp. 14-24) by permission of the author and the Graduat Program in Librarianship, Kansas State Teachers College, Empori. Kansas.

rather than with apologies; that the word "only" should be dropped from the all-too-frequent disclaimer, "I'm only a librarian," and that not until we ourselves recognize the importance of our calling will we be able to expect such recognition from others. I deplored the tendency of many librarians to defend their choice of a career on the grounds that it is so much fun, because it seems to me that librarianship is so much more than that, that the pleasure we get from it goes without saying. Our social value gives us satisfaction and fulfillment (not just fun), and I think we do the profession of librarianship a disservice when we minimize what librarianship does for other people to concentrate on what it does for us.

I think I can make my point most clearly by taking a really searching look at the one task of librarianship for which every librarian, whether in a special library, a university library, the public library or a children's collection is held responsible: the practice of book selection. For it is here that we exert, however indirectly, our greatest influence on the public we serve and the total society of which that public is a part. For one of the most important factors in determining what people will read, listen to, and watch, is Accessibility—having the material ready to hand. It is a factor which has been shown to be even more important than the reader's own professed interest in most cases of free-choice selection of communication experiences. There are few instances where the individual is so interested in a particular book that he will walk a mile, wait a week, or brave a storm for it. If he can't get the specific item he will take what is there. And when his interest is *more* general, which is frequently the case, when he just wants a good book to read or some general information on a broad subject—he certainly will select from what is available. The librarian, by determining what shall be available through the library, defines the field from which the average reader will make his choice.

It is my claim that this is an important responsibility—and that the librarian has discharged it (and will continue to discharge it) with a great deal more insight, tolerance, and efficiency than could a person with another kind of training. One has only to compare the quality and the variety of materials available through the average (not even the best, but just the average) public library, with that made available through any of the other communication agencies serving the public at large; the news stand, the radio and TV station, the moving picture theatre, and even most book stores.

One frequently hears the question—and the reason I'm holding forth in this vein today is that one frequently hears it from librarians themselves: "But who are we to decide what the patrons of the library should read?" The answer to that question is, obviously: "You are the librarians." Nobody—but nobody—is better qualified to make that decision. The library and the attainment of its objectives are the responsibility of the head librarian. In larger systems he delegates aspects of that responsibility to the other librarians on his staff. They are accountable to him; he is accountable to the public. If there is an abrogation of this accountability anywhere along the line then our claims to professional status are without foundation. *Not* to decide what the patrons of the library should read is not to be the librarian at all.

Now the librarian is quite right in pointing out that he cannot be an expert in all subject fields; that the authenticity, truth, and sincerity of certain works in subject fields in which he is not an expert can be established only by the experts in those fields. But the librarian is—or should be—the expert on the state of his library book collection and its adequacy for serving the needs of its patrons. Whether a certain book is needed in the library—quite apart from the enthusiastic endorsement of someone with a vested interest in it—is the decision the librarian must make.

To buy or not to buy—that is the question. Only the librarian really knows anything about the kinds of books that are needed for different kinds of readers; only the librarian knows what the present collection in the field is like and what gaps need to be filled; only the librarian knows what in the collection has been useful in the past, and what is being called for now. And most important of all—and this is a point about which I feel very strongly—only the librarian, of all the subject experts you can name, has that breadth of view which sees books in relation to the needs of others, all others, and not just to the particular subject specialty he himself professes. Advice from non-librarians can be very useful; much of it can and should be followed, but to decide whether to follow it or not—all things considered—is the librarian's assignment.

"All things considered" is the key phrase and it is in relation to it that the librarian stands head and shoulders above other experts whose subject specialization defines the limit of their attention. Any librarian who has ever relied upon the assistance of outside experts, or who has accepted suggestions from patrons, has run into the complete indifference and the complete ignorance they exhibit of fields outside their own special interests. If you wish to test my assumption here, take any authoritative subject expert you choose, and show him the list of titles in the "Weekly Record" of the *Publishers' Weekly*. It is my firm belief that, as he goes down the list, he will say much more frequently than any librarian ever would, "Who'd ever want to read something like that?" For the librarian is, in the familiar phrase, "a specialist in the general," and it is this specialization which is his particular strength, the key to his contribution, and the safeguard he provides for the preservation of the library's unique role in promoting freedom of inquiry.

This broad awareness of the many potential users for whom the librarian chooses books is absolutely essential in the selection process for the general library. And because it is, I believe that many of the library schools may be making a serious tactical mistake in basing their book selection courses on the premise that book selection for the library should be approached as though it were like the work of the literary critic. Many practicing librarians continue after library school to cling to this theory also, even though all of their experience tells them differently. It would help a great deal, I think, if librarians made their analogy, not with the work of the literary critic, but with the work of the responsible publisher. For the critic is fundamentally concerned with the book's adherence to a set of standards primarily literary; ideally his evaluation should be of the book for its own sake and in its own terms rather than for the sake of its users and in terms of its social utility.

On the other hand, what does a publisher do? He tries to meet the needs of *readers*—a variety of readers with a variety of interests and backgrounds—with books of quality. He tries to keep his list broad, and he is content to satisfy immediate needs as well as long-term ones. He is glad when he can publish a permanent classic, but he does not insist that all the books he publishes be classics. There are books of value as information, as recreation, as tools of education which may well be superseded in fifty years, or ten, or five, or one, which nevertheless deserve the chance to have their say now. He exists to serve, not only the particular demands of Art, but the individual and group demands of Tom, Dick and Harry. And thus the definition of "quality" in the publisher's vocabulary has connotations quite different from those carried by the term in the critic's lexicon.

A perfect example of this conflict in meaning was apparent in a University of Chicago Round Table broadcast a few years ago which featured the ALA's list of notable books. The chairman of the notable books committee was on the panel, as was a professor of literature in the College of the University. And it soon became abundantly clear that whereas both were using the phrase "notable books," they were not at all talking about the same things. By the definition of the term as used by the professor of literature there were not likely to be fifty notable books in the past twenty-five years. By the librarian's definition, the limitation to only fifty books was a stringent restriction when one considers the output of any one year. The professor never did seem to understand why the panelists, although they were talking to each other, were not communicating. But the librarians here, I am sure, can see what the trouble was immediately. For we know that the books that are selected as notable for the annual list are not necessarily monumental in the history of human thought. They are useful, they are well written, they are of value to our readers. Is this not indeed notable?

Do not be pushed by this anecdote into imagining that somehow the "quality" definition of the librarian is not really as good as that of the professor. The standards are different, not because the librarian is less serious in his approach to books, but because his aims are different. The librarian cannot be content with reaching a small, selective group of highly motivated readers with an intensive analysis of a few prescribed texts. The library is expected to have these, of course, but it is also expected—even by the college professor —to have the supplementary materials, the non-required readings, the books which will meet the needs of a lifetime of reading, not just those of the quarter, the semester, or the term. The professor has the freedom to work intensively with a limited selection of books precisely because the library exists—to broaden the reading interests of his students outside the classroom.

More importantly, of course, the public library serves many other readers besides the small group in the classroom; for many people it is a substitute for the kind of introduction that the classroom provides; for many others it is not related to classroom kinds of interests at all. Each of these groups is of equal importance in the eyes of the librarian, and this is what I meant when I said that only the librarian has the particular breadth of view necessary to make the final decisions about book purchase. For the college professor thinks in terms of his course objectives; the scholar in terms of his research aims; the subject expert in terms of the specialist's highly intensive needs. But the librarian thinks in terms of his publics—and notice that the word is plural.

It is important to emphasize the plural form of the word, because a trap into which librarians sometimes fall is to accept the mass medium notion that the "public" is a kind of single entity. It is not, of course, and because it is not, the library must diligently work to perform the individualized service which the mass media ignore. Most of the other media of communication today deliberately design their services to fit an audience—vast, undifferentiated, faceless audience. The library still serves the individuals who make up the audience and they are all different. This is a most important distinction to preserve; if ever we lose that, the brave new world of 1984 will really have arrived.

To many—and again, strangely enough, this seems to be true of some librarians as well as laymen—the provision of materials on all sides of an issue, the inclusion of all kinds of subject matter, and the receptability to the unpopular things as well as to the popular ones is seen as the absence of selection. Selection is interpreted to mean the careful elimination of some points of view and the complete provision of others. But a much more complicated job of selection is involved in the building of a collection on the basis of some kind of qualitative standards which will represent a great variety of interests, opinions and attitudes. This is real selection, for it involves professional judgment rather than mere recognition of subject content. It requires search to uncover the several kinds of materials which will guarantee the broad coverage we seek. It requires critical analysis to compare different treatments of similar topics and to select from them those which will represent fairly, and on a certain quality level, the different points of view which deserve a hearing. It requires control and broadmindedness to recognize the value of a viewpoint with which one disagrees, and to anticipate interest in areas which are new or of limited appeal or downright unpopular. For the provision of all points of view is not the same thing as the provision of "everything;" it means the selection of representative sampling of "everything"—which is quite a delicate and much more difficult process. More than that, the obligation of the librarian implies the imposition of a qualitative standard—not just representation of all points of view, but the best representative that can be found for each. How can this be designated the absence of selection?

Now the exercise of selection is forced upon the librarian whether or not he wishes to accept the responsibility it entails. Ideally he might wish that the principle of providing all points of view could be carried to its logical extreme to mean providing every book. Unfortunately the laws of physics make this ideal—supposing it were desirable—

impossible practically. No library in the world is large enough to house even one copy of every printed publication, and since in order to serve its publics, the library must have more than one copy of many of the books, we must defer to the limitations of space and eliminate some books from our collections.

But physical limitations, real as they are, are of secondary importance, as any practicing librarian knows. Few public librarians have as much as $2 per year to spend for each person in the community, and this will not buy many books even in inexpensive formats. But the librarian is charged with the responsibility of having available the more expensive rather than the less expensive books: the reference works, the illustrated volumes, the many volumed sets, the serious works of limited appeal. So again the librarian must select; 1000 new titles, let us say, from the more than 11,000 published (in the U.S. alone) in a single year.

I should think that the librarian would embrace the challenge which selection implies. If building a library collection meant merely to place a standing order for one copy of each title published, the librarian would need to be only a book-keeper, not a keeper of books. But a library is more than an indiscriminate conglomeration of print; it is an agency with a specific purpose: the enlightenment and improvement of its community. The library virtually by definition is destined to be selective.

The nature of the selection is also in a way predestined. For one thing, libraries are not—as are the other agencies and channels for the dissemination of ideas—money making enterprises. If twice as many books were to circulate this month as circulated last, not a single additional cent would be added to the library's coffers. Thus the library need not worry about pleasing the greatest possible number of readers, or increasing its Hooper rating, or swelling the box office take. Ideas can be evaluated as ideas rather than as gimmicks; values can be judged on other bases than dollar and cents return. To stay in business, the other agencies of communication usually feel that they must reflect the most widely popular notions and avoid controversy or challenge. The library is the only agency which is so organized and so privileged that it can do just the opposite. And I suggest that, in order for the library to justify its continuation in business, it has an obligation to do that which none of the other agencies can do: be better than the common denominator.

For it is important to remember that a reader learns, not only from the facts presented, but from the manner of presentation. If we make available to our citizens the second rate, the diluted, the inadequate, we are weakening their ability to distinguish between the meretricious and the valuable, the banal and the creative, the false and the true. Thus it is not enough that all sides be represented, but that they be represented by a presentation, the form and manner of which is in itself enlightening.

Remember that those of us who provide communication to the public are helping to create public demand for the kind of content we make available. Meeting public demand is not the simple one-way process we sometimes claim. People learn to like what they get—and if what they get is second rate, those who provide it are more at fault than the public whose second rate taste they condemn. How often have we, as enlightened citizens, attacked those who control the content of the mass media for their failure to exercise a "proper" control? How often have we condemned the sensational press, and asked why editors do not take a greater responsibility for selecting the matter which shall be emphasized and the manner in which news is presented? How often have we condemned the low level sameness of films, radio, and TV—and demanded that those in control take greater responsibility for elevating quality and introducing variety, even though vast audiences do not demand it? In so doing we are not attempting to curtail the freedom of the press. We are not advocating that news be suppressed, that entertainment be abandoned, or that popular interests be ignored. We are asking merely that those with authority accept responsibility.

I submit, that as librarians, our authority, and therefore our responsibility, are as great. For the reader who chooses his reading from what we make available to him can get the second rate from us only if we have it. A process of selection by the librarian should take place before the process of selection by the patron.

It is at this point that the analogy with publishing becomes even more clear. You will remember that I suggested that the librarian's selection obligations are like those of a "responsible" publisher, with responsible underlined. While the general publisher is anxious to serve the many interests of his potential readers, and while he is quite willing to select materials at a great many levels of profundity, difficulty, erudition, and permanent worth, he also has the obligation to impose standards upon his selection. We do not consider it wrong for the editor of *Harper's Magazine* to reject a manuscript on the ground that its proper market is *Confidential.* As a matter of fact we would consider him to be a very poor publisher indeed if he indiscriminately accepted for publication anything that anyone might under any set of conceivable circumstances wish to read. The editor—the publisher—has a public service to perform, and the public he wishes to serve is certainly as broad as possible. But this does not mean that he is obliged, on the basis of his public service obligations, to have something for everybody no matter how substandard some of the tastes to which he caters. An even more important public service to perform than the provision of something for everybody, is the imposition of standards.

So it is with the librarian. The stamp of the library's name on page 99 is like the publisher's imprint on the title page: it is, in effect, a kind of seal of approval by those experts who have been appointed to their positions because they are deemed to be capable of judging a book's worth. We abrogate our responsibility and are untrue to the public service ideal if we give that stamp to books that do not deserve it.

This, of course, is what makes book selection a professional process and not a clerical routine. And it is this—the emphasis on the positive rather than on the negative—which makes it selection and not censorship. It is not easy—and it may even lead to as many problems as it solves. For every selection we make—and more especially every rejection we make—is sure to render someone unhappy. Standards of quality, no matter how carefully arrived at, are still dependent upon subjective factors which may or may not be shared by all members of the community we serve. But the responsibility of leadership always entails this kind of problem. So long as we accept the necessity for making decisions at all (and that is what a professional person does), we must be prepared for the disagreement to which our decision is bound to give rise in some quarters. If we do not buy a book for good and sufficient reasons, we make unhappy the potential borrower who wanted to read it. And if, giving in to pressures from him, we add the book to the collection, we make unhappy those borrowers who agree with our original good and sufficient reasons. It is my belief that our position is strongest if we stand on our good and sufficient reasons—and that means, of course, that we ought to have a good reason for every decision we make, either to accept or reject.

The reasons may be of many kinds: selection is not based on the simple either/or which usually characterizes the discussions about selection. It is not a matter of having either important books or popular ones—we should have both, and sometimes they are the same books. It is not a matter of having a serious book or a recreational book—we should have both and sometimes *they* are the same books. It is not a matter of serving this public or that public—we should serve them all. But much as it may seem that we are by such reasoning sanctioning the inclusion of anything, remember that the standards we establish still must be imposed upon this variety of selections. Whatever the purposes we wish to serve by our book collection—and there are many of them—we must try to make sure that we are serving them with the best books for the purpose and not mediocre or poor ones.

The identification of the mediocre or poor book is not limited to literary criteria alone, although literary criteria are important. There are reasons why a public library should have some books which would not be on the reading list of a college course in literature. The library wishes to help meet some of the everyday practical needs of a great variety of readers: thus reliable and informative how-to-do-it books of all kinds have a logical place in our collections. The library wishes to provide insights into current problems and mores: thus a great many books which are reportage rather than history, journalism rather than sociology, have a logical place in our collections. The library wishes to help people understand themselves and those around them: thus a great many books of popular as well as academic psychology have a logical place in our collections. If a book has the power to provoke thought in the reader (as for example do books as widely divergent as *The Voices of Silence* and *The Insolent Chariots*); if it is of some significance in social or literary history (as are the works of the Beat Generation and the Angry Young Men); if it provides factual information in a context which sharpens its meaning and relevance to the life of today (something let us say, like Stuart Chase's *Some Things Worth Knowing*); if it is distinguished by the quality of its insights into human character (and here we might well raise the question of *Lolita,* no matter how distasteful we may find the insights to be); if it has the ability to recreate vividly a time, place, attitude, or way of life (as does a good history or even a good travel book); or if indeed it carries the reflection of a sharp and witty mind (not only that of a Spinoza but also that of a Jean Kerr or a Stephen Potter), then certainly it demands that we give it serious consideration for inclusion in our collections. If we can give a positive yes to any one or any combination of the above characteristics, we are on pretty strong ground for defending our choices. Note that we do not reject a book which cannot meet all of these criteria, but surely it should meet at least one. If it does not, I should think we need not be too embarrassed if the book does not appear in our collections, even if a public demand arises for it. Since we can't have everything, everything we have should be defensible.

It is clear, I suppose, that I am implicitly arguing for a statement of book selection policy: a clearly stated listing of the standards which govern the choices the library makes. One of the main reasons why book selection is difficult is that we are often called upon to justify it; it would not be difficult at all if we never had to answer for our decisions. When we are thus called upon, a forthright statement of the principles that guided us is an indispensable backstop. Do not for a moment imagine that it will necessarily satisfy those who raise the question, but it will certainly help to keep the level of the discourse on the points at issue, and not on irrelevancies.

The points at issue should be the objectives which your library aims to foster, and the contribution that your book selection makes to the achievement of those objectives. Or—to state that fancy phraseology in more commonplace terms —the librarian ought to know what he is doing and why.

What he is doing—it seems to me—is bringing all of his special expert knowledge to bear on the provision of reading and other materials of communication which will serve the needs and the interests of the community he or she serves. These needs are not always openly expressed; part of the librarian's problem is to discover the needs of the community which the members of the community themselves have not recognized. The reverse of the problem is even harder: to know when an expressed demand does not serve the community's true interest.

In other words, while demand is an important factor in library book selection, certain criteria of quality and value may outweigh demand in the final decision. Remember that a demand made in public is not necessarily evidence of a public demand; the influence of a single person, or a small number of vocal patrons, may give the effect of a great spontaneous movement. But even if the spontaneous movement does appear, the librarian should heed it only if he is convinced that it expresses needs that his library exists to serve. There are many needs in the community—even some reading needs —that may not be the library's obligation to meet.

On the other hand, be careful to avoid the snobbish notion that "popular" must of necessity be somewhat different from "good." We have fallen into a bad habit of equating "best seller" with pot-boiler; of assuming that anything which is liked by a great number of people must inevitably be less good than something with a narrower appeal. We sometimes forget that the best seller lists have carried first rate writers as well as third rate ones; we should remember that Dickens, Twain, Zola, Tolstoy, Wells, Cather, Toynbee, Hemingway, Faulkner are not of less value because they reached a wide readership.

In other words, popular demand in itself is really not a good enough reason either to purchase or to reject; it is merely one consideration among many that must be taken into account when the merits of any individual title are being weighed.

You will notice that in one way or another, we constantly come back to the same conclusion: the librarian must be a person capable of making decisions on the basis of informed judgments, and with the courage to stand back of his decision once he has made them. It is this that makes librarianship a true profession and not just a skilled trade: the fact that it calls for judgment, decision, responsibility; that it is dedicated to high standards of performance; and that it is based upon a code of ethical practice devoted to service to others. Of course it is difficult, and demanding, and challenging—would you really have it otherwise?

I hope not. The day may not yet be gone, but let us all do everything we can to hasten its going, when the appeal of librarianship is that it is such nice, clean, ladylike, undemanding work. I like to think that the appeal of librarianship to the young people of today is not that but this: its ideal of service, its importance in the fight for freedom of expression, its position of leadership and educational force in its community. To be a part of that kind of social contribution will inevitably require trouble and effort, but it is well worth it.

□

THE MISSION OF THE LIBRARIAN

José Ortega y Gasset

I would like to warn you initially that what you are about to read does not exactly coincide with the title given to my speech, a title which I encountered upon reading the program of this congress. I make this a matter of note, because this title—*The Mission of the Librarian*—is enormous and frigtening, and simply to accept it would be extremely pretentious. I could not pretend to reach the complex techniques of librarianship which for me are hermetic mysteries.

Even the word "mission" frightens me a little if I find myself obliged to use it in its full significance. The same applies to innumerable words of which we make daily use. If they suddenly began to function in the fullness of their true meanings, if upon our pronouncing and hearing them our minds understood at once their essential meanings, we would be frightened in the presence of the basic dramas which they contain.

THE PERSONAL MISSION

In order to demonstrate this with an example, it will be sufficient to look for a moment into the word "mission." Mission means, first of all, that which a man has to do with his life. Apparently, then, mission is something exclusive to man. Without man there is no mission. But the necessity expressed by the words "have to do" is a very strange condition and does not at all resemble the compulsion by which the stone gravitates towards the center of the earth. The stone cannot refuse to fall, but a man might very well not do that which he "has to do." Is this not curious? Here "necessity" is a thing most opposed to constraint—it is rather an invitation. Could anything be more gallant? Man finds himself invited to lend his consent to necessity. A stone, were it half-intelligent, might say upon observing this, "What good fortune to be a man! I have no choice but to fulfill my inexorable law: I must always fall. But what a man has to do or has to be is not imposed upon him, but proposed to him." But this imaginary stone would think thus because it was only half-intelligent. If it were completely so, it would see that this privilege of man's is a terrifying one. For it implies that at every moment of his life a man finds himself facing the various possibilities of acting and being, and that it is he alone who, consulting his unique responsibility, must decide in favor of one of them; that in order to decide to do this and not that, he must, whether he wishes to or not, justify the choice in his own eyes. That is, he must discover among the actions possible at that moment the one that possesses the most meaning, the one that is most his own. If he does not choose that one, he knows that he has deceived himself, falsified his own reality, and annihilated a moment of his vital time. There is no mysticism in what I say: it is evident that one cannot take a single step without justifying it before his own intimate tribunal. And so each of our acts must be drawn from the total anticipation of our destiny, the general program of our existence. This is true not only of the honest and heroic man, but also of the perverse and wicked. For the wicked man, too, is obliged to justify his acts in his own eyes and to find for them a meaning and a role in some program of life. Otherwise he would remain motionless, paralyzed like Buridan's ass.

Among the few papers that Descartes left after his death there was one written when he was twenty in which we read: *"Quod vitae sectabor iter?"* What way shall I choose in my life? This is a quotation taken from a verse of Ausonius, who in turn was translating an old Pythagorean poem entitled *De ambiguitate eligendae vitae*—concerning the perplexity in the choice of life.

Apparently man receives the inescapable impression that his life, and consequently his being, is something that he must choose. This is a stupefying fact, for it means that man—differing from all other entities of the universe which have their beings fixed in advance and exist precisely because of that—man is the unique and almost inconceivable reality who exists without having his being irremediably prefixed, who is not from the beginning what he is, who must choose his own being. And how shall he choose it? While calling to mind and considering the various kinds of life possible to him, a man observes that one of them attracts him more than the others —draws him, claims him, calls to him. This appeal that a certain kind of life has for us, this imperative cry, is called vocation.

In vocation, what is necessary for a man to do is not imposed upon him, but proposed to him. That is why life takes on the character of the realization of an imperative. It depends upon us to wish or not to wish to realize it, to be faithful or unfaithful to our vocation. But the vocation itself is not in our hands. That is why every human life has a mission. A mission is just this: the consciousness that every man has of his most authentic being, of that which he is called upon to realize. The idea of mission is, therefore, a constitutive ingredient of the human condition; and as I said a while ago, without man there is no mission. We may now add that without mission there is no man.

THE PROFESSIONAL MISSION
It is too bad that we cannot now go deeply into this subject,

one of the gravest and most fertile that exists: that of the relationship between man and his duty. For life is, before anything, something to do, a task. We do not give life to ourselves, life has been given to us. We encounter ourselves in its midst without knowing how or why. But that which has been given to us—life—now reveals itself as something we must make for ourselves, each man his own. In other words, to live we must always do something, under penalty of dying. Yes, life is a task; it gives us much to do, and the most important matter is to strike upon what is necessary to do. To this purpose we look around us at our social environment, and we find that it is made of a tissue of typical lives, lives that have certain general lines in common: we find doctors, engineers, professors, physicists, philosophers, laborers, manufacturers, salesmen, soldiers, masons, cobblers, teachers, actresses, dancers, nuns, dressmakers, ladies of society. At first we do not see the individual life of each doctor and each actress, but only the generic and schematic architecture of each life. The lives differ one from the other by the predominance of a type of work—for example, what the soldier does and what the scholar does. These schematic trajectories of life are the professions, careers, or beaten tracks of existence that we find already established, defined, and regulated in our society. We then choose from among them the one that will be our own, our *curriculum vitae.*

This has happened to you also. At that moment when a man makes his most decisive resolutions more or less clearly, you have found in your social environment, outlined before your arrival, the way of life and the mode of being human which is that of a librarian. You did not have to invent it: it was already there, in the society to which you belong.

At this point we must go a little more slowly. I have just said that the way of life and the type of human task that is the librarian's existed before any of you, that it sufficed for you to look around you to find it, already representing the lives of many men and women. But this has not always been true. There have been epochs in which there were no librarians, although there were books—not to speak of those other

long epochs when there were no librarians because there were
no books. Does this mean that in those times when there
were no librarians, although there were books, no men existed who occupied themselves with books in a way quite similar to that which constitutes your profession today? Undoubtedly there were people who were not content merely to
read books, but who collected, arranged, and catlogued them,
who took care of them. But had you been born in one of
those times you would have looked around yourselves in vain,
you would not have recognized in what these people did
what we today call librarianship. Their conduct would have
seemed to you what in fact it was—a singular, altogether personal mode of conduct, an individual trait, like the sound of
one's voice or the harmony of his gestures. The proof of this
is that at the death of these individuals, their occupation died
with them, was not practiced above and beyond the individual lives which exercised it.

What I mean to imply here will become quite clear if we
go to the other extremity of the development and ask ourselves: what happens today when a man who governs a public
library dies? He leaves an empty place behind him; his occupation continues intact in the form of an official post which
the state, the community, or some such corporation sustains
by their collective will and power, even though it may be
momentarily unoccupied and a salary continues to be assigned to this empty post. It follows that today the occupation of
collecting, arranging, and cataloging books is no longer a
purely individual pursuit but a post, a *topos,* a social position,
independent of individuals, sustained, acclaimed, and decided
by society as such, not simply by the occasional vocation of
one person or another. That is why today we find the care of
books impersonally established as a career or profession, and
upon looking around us we see it clearly and solidly defined,
like a public monument. Careers and professions are types of
human tasks which society needs. One of these tasks has
been, for some two centuries, that of the librarian. Every
society of the West today needs a certain number of doctors,
magistrates, soldiers, and librarians—to cure their citizens

when sick, to administer justice to them, to defend them, and to make them read.

And now here is the same expression which I used a while ago, this time applied to society instead of to the individual man. For society, also, it is *necessary* to do certain things. It, too, has its system of necessities, of missions.

We find ourselves, then—and this is more important than perhaps one imagines—in the presence of a duality: the mission of the man, that which a man must do in order to be what he is, and the professional mission, in this case the librarian's mission, or what a librarian must do in order to be a good librarian. It is very important not to confuse the one with the other.

Originally all that which today constitutes a profession, trade, or office was the creative inspiration of a man who felt the radical need of dedicating his life to an occupation hitherto unknown, who invented a new task. His mission was that which was necessary to him. This man died and his mission died with him. But after a time the community decided that this occupation or something which resembled it was necessary in order that society subsist and flourish. For example, there was once in Rome a man of the *gens Julia* whose name was Caius and whose surname was Caesar, and who had the idea of doing things no one had done before—among others, of proclaiming the right of Rome to the exclusive command of the world and the right of an individual to the exclusive command of Rome. This cost him his life. But a generation later Roman society felt, as a society, the need of someone doing again what Caius Julius Caesar had done. Thus it was that the void this man had left behind him, this empty design of his personal profile, found itself objectified, depersonalized into a magistracy, and the word "Caesar," which had designated an individual mission, came to designate a collective necessity. But notice the profound transformation which a type of human task undergoes when, instead of a personal necessity or mission, it becomes a collective necessity, an office or profession. In the first case, a man does what he and he alone must do, freely, and according to his exclusive responsibility. On the other hand, when this man practices a profession he engages himself to the needs of society. He then has to renounce a good part of his liberty; he finds himself obliged to set aside his individuality. He cannot determine his actions exclusively according to his personal point of view, but according to a collective one, under pain of being a bad professional and of suffering the grave consequences that society, which is very cruel, imposes upon those who serve it badly.

Perhaps an example will clarify what I imply here. If a fire breaks out in a house where a man lives with a number of other people, he might, in the extremity of despair, content himself with the idea of his own body in cinders and make no effort to put out the fire. But if by chance he survives, and it is evident that he could have put out the fire that has cost so many lives, society will castigate him, because he has not done that which he ought to have done socially, that is to say for the collective, not the individual, necessity. The professions always represent this type of duty for those who practice them. Like the fire, they are inescapable urgencies which the social situation presents and which we must attend to, whether we wish to or not. That is why they are called *offices,* and all the duties of the state are especially qualified as *official*—for in the state society shows itself superlatively emphasized, sharply defined, one might say exaggerated.

Linguists encounter some difficulty in affixing the etymology of this word "official," a word by which the Latins designated duty. This is because, as often happens, they do not properly conceive the original, vital situation to which the word corresponds and in which it was created. But there is no semantic difficulty in recognizing that *officium* comes from *ob* and *facere.* The prefix *ob* generally means to go out promptly to encounter something, in this case a task. *Officium* means, then, to do without hesitation or delay the urgent duty, the task presented as inescapable.[1] Is this not what constitutes the very idea of society? When we are presented with something as a duty, it is made clear that we have no margin in which to decide for ourselves whether or not it

ought to be done. We may do it or not, but the fact that it
ought to be done is indisputable—for such is duty. All this
tells us that in order to determine the mission of the librarian
we must begin, not with the man who practices the profession, his tastes, peculiarities, and suitabilities, nor with an
abstract ideal which presumes to define once and for always
what a library is, but with the social necessity which your
profession serves. And that necessity, like everything else that
is properly human, does not consist of a fixed magnitude; on
the contrary, by its very essence it is variable, migratory,
evolutionary—in short, historical.

HISTORY OF LIBRARIANSHIP: THE 15th CENTURY

If you will examine it now you will observe how clearly the
duty of the librarian has varied in direct proportion to the
significance of the book as a social necessity.

If it were possible to reconstruct the past exactly, we
would discover with surprise that the history of librarianship
shows us transparently the most secret intimacies of the
evolution which the Occidental world has undergone. This
would prove that we had envisioned the profession of the librarian, apparently so specialized and eccentric, in its effective and fundamental reality. When we envision anything
whatever in its reality, no matter how diminutive and sub-
ordinate, it puts us in contact with all other realities, places
us in the center of the world, and shows us in every direction
the unlimited and pathetic perspectives of the universe. But, I
repeat, we cannot even now begin that profound history of librarianship. That task remains for someone better gifted than
I to undertake.

The functional relationship between what the librarian
has done in each epoch and the significance of the book as a
necessity among Occidental societies seems to me to be
unquestionable.

For the sake of brevity, let us pass over Greece and
Rome. That which was a book to them is a very strange thing
to us, if described with precision. We shall speak only of the
new populations who initiated a new growth upon the ruins

of Greece and Rome. When, then, do we see the human figure
of the librarian outlined for the first time against the social
scene? When would a contemporary, in looking about him,
have been able to find the silhouette of the librarian, a clearly
defined public figure? Without doubt, at the beginning of the
Renaissance. And take note, a little before printed books existed! During the Middle Ages the care of books was still
infrasocial, not showing itself in public view; it was still la-
tent, secret, one might say intestine, confined in the secret
precincts of the cloisters. Even in the universities the practice
was not outstanding. They no doubt kept the books necessary for the business of teaching, no more, no less, just as one
keeps enough utensils for housekeeping. The guarding of
books was not a special task. It was not until the dawn of the
Renaissance that the pattern of the librarian's work distinguished itself from the other general ways of life and appeared in public view. And—note this coincidence—it was just at
this epoch also that for the first time the book, in the strict
sense of the word—not the religious book nor the book of
law, but the book written by an author, the book that is only
a book, not a revelation or a code—it was just at this epoch
that the book was first socially felt as a necessity. Long before this time, no doubt, one individual or another had felt
this need of books, but more as a personal desire or pain, on
his own account and at his own risk. At the time of which I
speak the individual had already discovered that he need not
experience this need by himself. He found it in the air, in the
atmosphere, a thing recognized, one did not know exactly by
whom; a need that seemed to be felt by "the others"—that
vague collectivity, that mysterious substratum of all society.
The attraction of the book, the hope invested in the book,
already these had ceased to be the concern of one or another
individual and possessed that anonymous and impersonal
character that belongs to every collective validity. History is
first of all the story of the emergence, development, and
decadence of these social validities: opinions, norms, prefer-
ences, negations, and fears which individuals find already
made in their social environment, and which they must take

into account whether they wish to or not, just as they must take physical nature into account. It does not matter whether the individual is in accord with these validities, for the effective vigor which they enjoy does not depend upon whether you and I give them our assent; on the contrary, it is when our dissent comes in conflict with their granite hardness that we best understand to what point they are effectively in force.

In this sense, then, I say that up until the Renaissance the need of books did not constitute a social validity in full force. It became one at that time. And that is why we now see the librarian emerge immediately as a professional. But we may be still more precise. At this epoch the need for books took on the nuance of faith in books. The revelations that God had given to man lost their efficacy. People began to have faith in all that man thinks with his reason alone, and consequently in all that man writes. What a strange and radical adventure for the Western world! And note how it sufficed for us merely to touch upon the history of librarianship in order to fall, as if through a trap-door, into the hidden depths of European evolution.

The social need for books consisted at that time merely of the need to have books—for there were few of them. In proportion to that need we see the corresponding growth of those librarians of genius who, during the Renaissance, deployed in the hunt for books unbelievable astuteness and tenacity. The compiling of catalogs was not yet an urgent affair. The acquisition and production of books, on the contrary, assumed heroic proportions. All this was in the fifteenth century.

It hardly seems due to pure chance that precisely in this epoch, when such a lively need for books was felt, printing was invented.

THE NINETEENTH CENTURY

Let us leap over three centuries and find ourselves in 1800. What has happened to books in the meantime? Many have been published; printing is no longer expensive. One no longer feels the lack of books, but the need to catalog them, there are so many. So much for the material quantity of books. As for their contents, the needs felt by society have also changed. Much of the hope founded upon books seems to have been realized. There are some things in the world that were not there before: the sciences of nature and history and much technical knowledge. The search for books has ceased to be a problem; there is now the problem of finding and encouraging readers. Libraries multiply at this stage, and with them the librarians. The role of the librarian has become a profession which occupies many men; but it is still a spontaneous, social profession. The state has not yet made it an official one.

The decisive step in the evolution of librarianship was taken a little later, toward 1850. The profession as a state office is not very old, then, and this detail concerning its age is of very great importance. Because history, everything historical—that is, everything human—is time in motion, and time in motion always means age. It follows that everything human is either in its infancy, its youth, its maturity, or its senility.

I am a little afraid at having pointed out this perspective to you for I fear that you are going to ask me with great curiosity in what age I think the profession is, and whether to be a librarian is to be, historically, young, mature, or aged. We shall see at the end whether I am able to give you some answer to this question.

But let us come back to the point of evolution where we were, to the moment when, approximately a century ago, the profession of librarian became an official one. No doubt you think, as I do, that the most important incident in the history of a profession is its passing from an occupation spontaneously favored by society, to a bureaucracy of the state. What is the cause of such an important change? Or at least, of what is it always a symptom? The state is also society, but not all of it. It is only a mode, or a part of it. Society, inasmuch as it is not the state, operates by the means of usage, custom, public opinion, language, etc.—in short, by the means of imprecise and diffuse validities. In the state, on the other hand, the effective vigor of everything social is raised to its highest power and becomes, so to speak, something solid, perfectly clear and precise. The state operates by the means of laws, terribly imperative announcements of an almost mathematical rigor. That is why I said a moment ago that the order of the state is the extreme form of the collective order, the superlative of the social. If we apply this to our present problem, we shall find that a profession does not become official and pass into the hands of the state until that moment when the collective need which it serves becomes extremely sharp and is no longer felt as a simple need but as an inescapable necessity, an urgency. The state does not admit superfluous occupations in its own orbit. Society feels at every moment that it has many things to do, but the state is careful to intervene only in those which apparently must be done. There was a time when the consultation of the auspices and other mysterious signs that the gods sent to their people were believed to be indispensable to the existence of society. That is why the ceremony of augury became an institution and an official duty, and the augurs and diviners formed an important bureaucracy.

The French Revolution, after its turbulent melodrama, had transformed European society. A so-called democratic body had succeeded the old aristocratic body. This society was the final consequence of the faith in books which had been felt in the Renaissance. Democratic society is a daughter of books, the triumph of the book written by man over the book revealed by God, over the book of laws dictated by the autocracy. The revolt of the people had been accomplished in the name of all the things that we call reason, culture, etc. These abstract entities came to occupy in men's hearts the same central position formerly occupied by God, an entity no less abstract. There is always a strange propensity in man to nourish himself, above all, in the abstract.

The fact is that toward 1840 books were no longer a necessity in the sense of an illusion or a hope, but God having departed and the traditional authority of divine right having evaporated, there remained no more ultimate appeal than the

book on which to found all that was social. It was therefore
necessary to take refuge in the book as in a rock of salvation.
The book became socially indispensable. This was the era in
which appeared the phenomenon of copious editions. The
masses threw themselves upon the volumes with an almost
breathless urgency, as though books were balloons of oxygen.
The consequence was that for the first time in Western history culture became a *raggione di stato*. The state made science and letters official. It recognized the book as a public
function and as an essential political organism. By virtue of
this, the profession of the librarian became a bureaucracy for
reasons of state.[2]

 We have come, then, in the process of history, in the
process of the human life of Europe, to the phase in which
the book has become an indispensable necessity. Without the
sciences, without the technologies, these societies so dense in
population and of such a high standard of living could not have
materially existed. Still less could they have lived morally
without a vast repertory of ideas. There was only one vague
possibility of making democracy effective: that the masses
cease to be masses by dint of gulping enormous doses of culture, an effective culture, be it understood, germinating in
each man, not merely received, heard, or read. The nineteenth century understood this from its beginning with perfect
clarity. It is an error to believe that this century could have
tried democracy without taking into account *a priori* that the
enterprise was very improbable. It saw perfectly what had to
be done—re-read St.-Simon, Auguste Comte, Tocqueville,
and Macaulay. It tried to do it. However, it is important to
recognize that it tried at first feebly and later frivolously.

 But let us leave this now and go to what is more important to us. We have come to a point that is going to demand
the most alert effort of attention, because the theme of the
book and the librarian which up until this point has been sustained with an almost idyllic mildness is going to be suddenly
transformed into a drama. And this drama, in my opinion, is
going to constitute the most authentic mission of the librarian. Until now we have only considered what that mission has

been; we have seen only the images of its past. Now the profile of a new task is going to rise before your eyes, a task incomparably higher, graver, more essential. One might say that until now the profession has lived only its hours of play and prelude—*Tanze und Vorspiel.* But now the serious part arrives, for the drama begins.

THE NEW MISSION

Until the middle of the nineteenth century our Western societies felt that the book was a need, but this need bore a positive sign. I shall clarify briefly what I mean by this expression.

This life that we encounter, that has been given to us, has not been given to us ready-made. We must make it for ourselves. This means that life consists of a series of difficulties that must be resolved. Some are physical, securing nourishment, for example; others are called spiritual, such as not dying of boredom. Faced with these difficulties, man reacts by inventing physical and spiritual instruments which facilitate his struggle against them. The sum of these facilities which man thus creates is culture. The ideas that we forge for ourselves concerning things constitute the best example of that arsenal of instruments which we interpose between ourselves and the difficulties around us. A clear idea about a problem is like some marvelous apparatus which transforms the painful difficulty into a comfortable facility. But ideas are fleeting; for a moment they illuminate our minds with magic clarity, but a moment after, that light is extinguished. Memory must make an effort to conserve them, but memory is not even able to conserve our own ideas, and it is extremely important to conserve those of other men. It is so important, that this is one of the most characteristic traits of our human conditions. The tiger today must remain the same tiger as if there had never been any other tigers before him; he does not profit from the thousands of experiences that other tigers have had in the sonorous depths of the forests. Each tiger is therefore a first tiger; he must start again from the beginning his profession of tiger. But the man of today does not begin by being a man. He inherits the forms of existence, the ideas, the vital experiences of his ancestors. He begins at a level represented by the human past accumulated beneath his feet. Faced with no matter what problem, man does not find himself alone with his personal reaction, with whatever idea occurs to him, but has at his disposal all or many of the ideas, reactions, and inventions which his ancestors have already found. That is why his life is made up of the accumulation of other lives and why his life is substantially a progress. We will not discuss here whether he progresses toward the better, toward the worse, or toward nothing at all.

It must be of singular importance, then, to add to this instrument, the idea, another instrument which solves the difficulty of preserving all the ideas. That instrument is the book. Inevitably, the more one accumulates of the past, the greater is the progress. And thus it has happened that scarcely had the technical problem of having books been resolved by the means of printing, than the movement of history and the speed of progress began to accelerate, attaining today a rhythm that seems to us vertiginous. What would the men of more leisurely ages have thought of it? For it is not only a matter of our machines which produce things at stupefying speeds, nor of our vehicles which transport our bodies with an almost mythological celerity; it is a matter of the total reality which is our life, of the composite volume of history which has prodigiously augmented the frequency of its mutations and consequently its absolute movement, its progress. And all this is principally due to the facility which the book represents.

Here is why our societies have felt the book as a necessity; it was the necessity of a facility, of a beneficial instrument. But imagine the instrument invented by man to render a dimension of existence easier, transforming itself into a new difficulty. Imagine this instrument turning against man, becoming uncontrollable and provoking morbid and unforeseen consequences. It will remain no less necessary, in the sense of facilitating the problem in view of which it was invented. But without ceasing to be necessary, and exactly because it is so necessary for this problem, it will add a new and unexpected anguish to our lives. Formerly it was a pure facility for us, and consequently represented in our lives a factor with a positive sign. Now its relationship with us becomes complicated, and it is charged with a negative sign.

This case is not purely hypothetical. Everything that man invents and creates to facilitate his life, everything that we call civilization and culture, reaches a point at which it turns against him. Precisely because it is a creation, it remains in the world, outside of the subject which created it. It enjoys its own existence, transforms itself into a thing, into a world which confronts man, and, thrust toward its own inexorable destiny, it becomes detached from the intention with which man had created it in order to escape from an occasional difficulty. This is the inconvenience of being a creator. This also happened to the god of Christianity: he created the angel with great mystical wings, and the angel revolted against him. He created man with no wings but the wings of imagination, but man also rebelled, revolted against him, and began to cause him difficulties. Cardinal Cusano said that man, being free, is a creator, but that he is free and a creator in the temporal instant, under the pressure of circumstance; for that reason he deserves the title of *Deus occasionatus,* a second-hand god. For that reason also, his creations turn against him. Today we live in an age extremely characteristic of this tragic situation. Economy, technology, all the facilities that man has invented today besiege him and threaten to strangle him. The sciences which have grown so fabulously, multiplying and specializing themselves, surpass the capacities of acquisition which man possesses. They torture and oppress him like the plagues of nature. Man is in danger of becoming the slave of his sciences. Study is no longer the *Otium* and the *Schole* as in Greece. Study is already beginning to inundate the life of man and to overflow its limits. The inversion characteristic of this revolt of human creations against their creator is already imminent. Man, instead of studying in order to live, soon must live in order to study.

Under one form or another, this has already happened

several times in history. Man loses himself in his own wealth: his own culture, proliferating like tropical vegetation around him, ends by smothering him. What we call the historical crises are finally nothing but this. Man cannot be too rich; if an excess of facilities and possibilities are offered for his choice, he comes to grief among them; and confounded with possibilities, he loses the sense of the necessary.[3]

This has been the perennial tragic destiny of the aristocracies: all of them finally degenerated because the excess of means and facilities atrophied their energies.

Are we going too far when we invite ourselves to reflect and ask ourselves whether Western societies are not already beginning to feel the book as an instrument in revolt, as a new difficulty? In Germany they are reading the book of Mr. Juenger in which one encounters sentences approximately like this: "It is a shame that we have come to this stage in our history without a sufficient number of illiterate people." You will tell me, perhaps, that this is an exaggeration. But let us not deceive ourselves. An exaggeration is always the extreme statement of something that is not in itself an exaggeration.

In all of Europe there exists the impression that there are too many books. It is the opposite of the Renaissance. The book has ceased to be an attraction and is felt instead as a heavy load. The man of science himself observes that one of the great difficulties of his work is to orient himself in the bibliography of his subject.

Let us not forget that always when an instrument created by man revolts against him, society in turn revolts against that creation, doubts its efficacy, feels an antipathy for it, and demands that it fulfill its primitive mission of pure facility.

Here then is the drama: the book is indispensable at this stage in history, but the book is in danger because it has become a danger for man.

One might say that human need ceases to be purely positive and begins to charge itself with negativity at the very moment when it begins to seem indispensable. Every human need, if it really is one, may in a sense be qualified as indispensable. This is obvious. But if we intend to obtain a clear concept of a need or necessity we immediately discover a double significance which must be given to the term "indispensable." I cannot go into the subject deeply at this moment, and I shall limit myself to transcribing a few lines from a course on "The Principles of Metaphysics" which I gave in 1933 at the University of Madrid, some parts of which have been published:

> I call human need all that which is felt as literally indispensable—that is, that which we believe we cannot live without—or rather that which, even though in fact we could do without it, continues to be felt by us as a void or defect in our lives. Thus, eating is a literally indispensable need. But being happy, and being so in a certain and precise manner, is also a need. No doubt we are not happy, and that is to say in fact that we do without happiness and live unhappily. But—and here is the point—the feeling of the need for happiness continues to be still active within us. Then one may object that being happy is not a need, it is a mere desire. In fact it is, but this reveals to us that so many of our desires are only desires, and consequently things that we can completely forego, and without this renunciation leaving any amputation or emptiness in our lives. There are other desires which *as desires* we cannot do without, and that is to say that although we may be forced to renounce their satisfaction in the reality which they desire, we still cannot stop desiring even if we want to. That is why they demand to be called needs.

It is not good, in fact, for a thing to be vigorously indispensable even if we possess that thing in abundance, and even if its use and profit do not cost us any new difficulty. The sole characteristic of indispensability makes us feel enslaved by it. In this sense one may say that social needs become properly affairs of the state when they have already become negative. That is why everything that concerns the state is sad and painful and there is no means of completely freeing it of its aspects of a hospital, a barracks, or a prison.

Nevertheless, the fully negative character surges up when

an instrument created as a facility spontaneously provokes an unforeseen difficulty and aggressively turns upon man. This is what is beginning to happen today with the book, and what has caused to disappear almost completely throughout Europe the ancient joy with which the printed page was welcomed.

All of this indicates to me that librarianship is entering its maturity. If life is a task, it follows that the different ages of life are distinguished by different styles in the activity of man. Youth generally does not do what it does because it ought to do it, because it considers it inexcusable not to do it. On the contrary, as soon as youth observes that a thing is necessary, indispensable, it tries to avoid it, and if it does not succeed, carries out its task in sadness and disgust. The lack of logic implied in this attitude belongs to that magnificent treasure of absurdity of which youth happily consists. The young man embarks with enthusiasm only upon tasks which are presented to him as revokable, in which there is no restraint, and which can be perfectly replaced by others no less opportune and laudable. The young man needs to think that at any moment, if he so wishes, he can abandon the task and jump to another one. He thus avoids the feeling that he is a prisoner of a single task. In short, the young man is not bound to what he does; or equally, though he fulfills it carefully and even heroically, he almost never takes his task with complete seriousness. In the secret depth of his soul he refuses any irrevocable engagement and prefers to conserve a permanent freedom to do something else, even the opposite of what he is doing. Thus, his concrete occupation appears to him as a simple example of innumerable other tasks to which he may at any moment dedicate himself. Thanks to this private ruse he virtually obtains his ambition: to do everything at once, to enjoy at one time all the modes of being human. There is no use to try to deny it—the young man is essentially disloyal to himself; he plays with his mission as a toreador plays with a bull. His activity retains something of the games of childhood, it is almost always a mere experiment, a test, a pattern of no value.

The age of maturity conducts itself in the opposite fashion. It feels the fruition of reality, and reality in a duty is exactly the opposite of caprice. It is that which one cannot either do or not do with complete indifference; it is that which seems inexcusable and urgent. At this age life arrives at its own truth and discovers this essential platitude: that one life cannot live all lives, but on the contrary each life consists of "unliving" all others and remaining alone with itself. This vivid consciousness of not being able to be or to do but one thing at a time purifies our demands of what that thing shall be. We then feel a repugnance for that juvenile narcissism which *does* no matter what, precisely because it *doesn't* matter what, and which nevertheless believes in its vanity that it is doing something. For the mature the only thing worth doing is that which is useless to avoid because it is inevitable; hence its preference for the problems which are problems in the superlative, that is to say problems which have become conflicts, necessities with a negative sign.

If we translate these distinctions between the ages in personal life into terms of collective life and of the professions, we shall discover that librarianship has reached the point where it.must confront the problem of the book as a species of conflict.

Here, then, is the point at which I see the new mission of the librarian rise up incomparably higher than all those preceeding. Up until the present, the librarian has been principally occupied with the book as a thing, as a material object. From now on he must give his attention to the book as a living function. He must become a policeman, master of the raging book.

THE BOOK AS A CONFLICT

The gravest negative attributes that we begin to perceive today in the book are the following:

1. There are already too many books. Even when we drastically reduce the number of subjects to which man must direct his attention, the quantity of books that he must absorb is so enormous that it exceeds the limits of his time

and his capacity of assimilation. Merely the work of orienting oneself in the bibliography of a subject today represents a considerable effort for an author and proves to be a total loss. For once he has completed that part of his work, the author discovers that he cannot read all that he ought to read. This leads him to read too fast and to read badly; it moreover leaves him with an impression of powerlessness and failure, and finally skepticism towards his own work.

If each new generation continues to accumulate printed paper in the same proportion as the last few generations, the problem posed by the excess of books will become truly terrifying. The culture which has liberated man from the primitive forest now thrusts him anew into the midst of a forest of books no less inextricable and stifling.

It would be useless to wish to resolve the conflict by supposing that the need to read the books accumulated in the past does not exist and that it is a matter of one of those innumerable commonplaces, empty of sense, invented by that bigotry of "culture" which was still in force in some minds a few years ago. The truth is just the opposite. Under the surface of our epoch there is already germinating, though some individuals have not yet perceived it, a new and radical imperative for the intelligence: the imperative of historical consciousness. The following conviction will soon arise with forceful evidence: that if man truly wishes to enlighten his being and his destiny he must attain to an historical consciousness of himself. That is to say, he must seriously begin to do with history that which toward 1600 he seriously began to do with physics, and that history will not be the Utopia of science which it has been until now, but an effective knowledge. In order that it may be such, many exquisite ingredients are necessary. One of these, the most obvious, is precision. This attribute of precision is a formal and extrinsic element of the first stages of a science when that science reaches the moment of its authentic constitution. The history that is to be made tomorrow will no longer speak so lightly of epochs and centuries. It will articulate the past into very brief stages of organic character, into generations, and it will try to define quite rigorously the structure of human life in each one of these stages. For this purpose it will not be content to emphasize one or two works which are arbitrarily qualified as "representative." It will be necessary to read really and effectively all the books of a determined time, to register the description of them most carefully, finally establishing what I would call a "statistics of ideas" in order to determine strictly the chronological moment at which an idea germinated, the process of its expansion, its exact duration as a collective validity, and then the hour of its decline, of its petrifaction as a simple commonplace, and finally its disappearance behind the horizon of historic time.

This enormous task can never be accomplished unless the librarian makes every effort to reduce the difficulty in the measure in which it is incumbent upon him, freeing from useless efforts the men whose sad mission is, and must be, to read many books, as many books as possible—the naturalist, the doctor, the philologist, the historian. It is necessary that the collection of descriptive and selective bibliography upon a given subject cease to be a problem for an author. That this has not already come to pass today seems incompatible with the accomplishment of our times. The economy of mental effort demands it urgently. It is necessary, then, to create a new bibliographic technique, one of vigorous automatic action. This technique will raise to its highest power the labor begun by librarians some centuries ago in the forms of catalogs.

2. But it is not only that there are too many books; they are being produced every day in torrential abundance. Many of them are useless and stupid; their existence and their conservation is a dead weight upon humanity which is already bent low under other loads. At the same time, it also happens that in all the disciplines one often regrets the absence of certain books, the lack of which holds up research. This fact is much more serious than the vague pronouncement leads one to suppose. It is incalculable how many important solutions upon the most diverse subjects never come to maturity because they encounter lacunae in previous research. The

excess and the lack of books are of the same origin: production is carried on without regimen, almost completely abandoned to spontaneous chance.

Is it too Utopian to imagine in a not too distant future
librarians held responsible by society for the regulation of the
production of books, in order to avoid the publication of
superfluous ones and, on the other hand, to guard against the
lack of those demanded by the complex of vital problems in
every age? All human tasks begin in a spontaneous and un-
regulated exercise; but also, when through their own extension they complicate and impinge upon one another, they
come to submit to organization. It seems to me that the hour
has arrived for the collective organization of book production; for the book itself, as a human modality, this organization is a question of life or death.

And let no one offer me the foolish objection that such
an organization would be an attack upon liberty. Liberty has
not come upon the face of the earth to wring the neck of
common sense. It is precisely because some have wished to
employ it in such an enterprise, because they have pretended
to make of it the chief instrument of madness, that liberty is
having a bad time in the world at present. The collective
organization of book production has nothing to do with the
subject of liberty, no more nor less than the need which has
demanded the regulation of traffic in the great cities of today. Moreover, this organization would not be of an authori-
tarian character, no more in fact, than the internal organization of works in a good academy of sciences.

3. Furthermore, the librarian of the future must direct
the non-specialized reader through the *selva selvaggia* of
books. He will be the doctor and the hygienist of reading. On
this point also we find ourselves in a situation quite the reverse of that in 1800. Today people read too much. The
condition of receiving without much effort, or even without
any effort, the innumerable ideas contained in books and
periodicals has accustomed the common man to do no thinking on his own account; and he does not think over what he
has read, the only method of making it truly his own. In

addition, there is that gravest and most radically negative character of the book, and we must dedicate our utmost effort of attention to it. A large part of today's terrible public problem proceeds from the fact that ordinary minds are full of ideas received in inertia, ideas half understood and deprived of their virtues. Ordinary minds are thus stuffed with pseudo-ideas. In this aspect of his profession, I imagine the librarian of the future as a filter interposed between man and the torrent of books.

In summation, to my mind the mission of the librarian ought to be, not as it is today the simple administration of the things called books, but the adjustment, the setting to rights, of that vital function which is the book. ☐

[1] The other meaning of *officium*—to place obstacles—though it seems to have a bellicose connotation, is related to the one already indicated. The urgent duty most characteristic of primitive life is the battle against the enemy, facing and opposing it. Thus it does not matter whether *officium* first means "to place obstacles" and later, by generalization, becomes the prototype of urgency, or whether, vice versa, duty in general becomes specialized to the more definite sense of opposition to the enemy.

It is a curious fact that the same idea of going promptly to some urgent duty also animates the word "obedience" which comes from *ob* and *audire*—that is to say, to immediately execute the order as soon as it is heard. In Arabic the expression which designates obedience is a combination of the two words "understood" and "done."

[2] The same process created the mandarins in China when there was no god nor any strong commandments.

[3] Chateaubriand, who had much more talent and profundity than is recognized by the ignorant literary criticism of the past eighty years, has already said, "The invasion of ideas has succeeded the invasion of the barbarians; today's civilization, decomposing, is losing itself in itself." *Memoires d'outre-tombe*, Ed. Bire, VI, 450.

THE MAGIC TRIAD:
BOOKS, PEOPLE, AND IDEAS

Richard Barksdale Harwell

In an age of specialization librarians are generalists. In an age
of mechanization they are humanists. In an age of conformity
they are individualists. It should not be otherwise. Librarianship is a young calling and an old trade. It is a young business
and an old love. It is an art in its ways of creating something
new from the work of the past and a craft in the systematic
techniques it must use. In a word, it is a profession.

Perhaps librarianship is not as well established as a profession as the triad of learned professions. But law, medicine,
and theology assume no loss of prestige by being younger
than the traditional "oldest profession." Librarianship is not
only an honored profession, it is a creative profession. Any
author is as indebted for the ideas he sets forth in his books
to the volumes of the past as he is to his own human ancestry
for his personality.

I remember the thrill of discovery (if that word can be
used in connection with assigned reading) that accompanied
my collegiate acquaintance with John Livingston Lowes' *The
Road to Xanadu*. This book traces the literary sources of
Coleridge's poem. Dr. Lowes found the raw material for
"Kubla Khan" in obscure and unexpected places, and demonstrated how the fabulously fecund mind of the poet worked a

a sort of sea-change on the facts he read and produced something new, a poem that is a wondrous fact itself. *The Road to Xanadu* was then already a famous book, but it was new to me. It caused all reading and scholarship to make new sense for me. And it caused libraries to make new sense for me—not as storehouses, but as treasuries of ideas.

Professor Raymond Irwin traces the story of libraries in a delightful essay, *The Golden Chain,* which was also his inaugural lecture as Professor of Library Studies at the University of London in 1957. Mr. Irwin rightfully recognizes the book as the focus of a library. He recognizes also the function of the librarian. "A library," he declares, ". . . is something much more than a shelf of books, or a press, or even a great book-lined reading room. Without its owner, without its users, it is dead. And so it is true to define a library as a community in which both reader and writer meet, to which both contribute something of value, mutually forging the links of the chain as it passes from mind to mind and from generation to generation. At the centre of this community, if the library be a great one, is the librarian. . . ."

The library, then, is a community of books and people and ideas. Perhaps it is not the history of libraries that is "the golden chain," but the meshing of relationships in this community. Perhaps it is not a chain at all, for in a chain the different parts are merely interlocked. Perhaps it is a golden rope in which ideas, books, and people are strands woven together to produce an entity stronger than its parts. It is the responsibility of librarians to so serve their profession that the weaving of these strands continues.

THE INFORMED GENERALIST

I believe in librarianship as a unity. I am proud to be a college and university librarian, but I believe in librarianship as a whole. I think all librarianship is a part of the same golden rope—and who is to measure which section of the rope is most important? I know that children's librarians, public librarians, school librarians, college and university librarians, special librarians of all sorts work with the same elements toward the same ends. All work with books, people, and ideas.

We have chosen a field in which we are by necessity, even by definition, generalists. Have we really set the informed generalist at the peak of our profession? In a few cases, yes. I can remind you of such librarians as Bill Dix at Princeton, Ralph Ellsworth at the University of Colorado, Robert B. Downs at the University of Illinois. But for every one of these informed generalists there are minor specialists by the score who fail to see the dignity and strength of their profession because they are blinded by the light they think they have seen in a specialty. We have graduated too many *petits fonctionnaires* into positions where a generalist—a librarian, if you will—is needed. Details of administration must be met. But there are more important things in librarianship. We usually have the good jugment to hire an architect to work with a librarian in the designing of a building. We are shocked when a library is set up as part of a business or research operation without a professional librarian to guide it. Is it too much to believe that a librarian might well have on his staff a management man to perform management functions? This would be no forfeit of right or responsibility. As an informed generalist the librarian would still direct policy.

The specialist is tremendously useful in a library. There are many special jobs to be done. But the direction of the library must be by a generalist. And I am somewhat afraid of the specialist anywhere. A reference librarian must know more than the answer to a specific question. A cataloger must know the library's catalog, the general personality of the library, and a great deal about it's goals to be a good cataloger. The circulation librarian who only hands out books is no librarian at all. The rare book librarian must not be permitted an ivory tower, but must be aware of the place of his collections in the scheme of his library. Even the non-professional assistants in a library must know it generally. Nobody, but nobody, on a library staff should ever have to shunt off a patron with a "that's-not-my-department" kind of answer.

What applies to the general administration of a library

applies even more strongly to the building of its book collections. Book selection is a complex process. The assets of the specialist can be put to good use, but the general direction must be by a generalist and, I believe, by a humanist. Great libraries are built in many different ways. Universities and the large research libraries must depend heavily on block purchases. The college library must select more specifically to its needs. But, in every case, the librarian is abdicating his proper position if he does not reserve for the library very close control of the selection for his collections.

The humanistic approach is the only professional attitude tenable for librarians. I believe this to be true in even the specialized scientific libraries. Scientific studies are currently and rightfully at the fore of our thinking, but the great scientists of the past have been humanists as well as technicians. We must keep it so.

I am openly suspicious — and privately, mildly enthusiastic — about the changes the documentalists, the communicators, the information retrievers promise for librarianship. Librarians are often more communicators than they are bookmen. If these things help in solidifying our magic triad of books, people, and ideas — good. But "communicator" has a mechanical connotation, or a connotation of pre-breakfast television; "librarian," through long usage, has a connotation of inclusive interest.

In specialized areas of research documentalists are undoubtedly useful. I persuade myself the documentalist is not an "anti-bookman" but a super bookman in a restricted field, a very special specialist who must know his subject area in minute detail. I argue with me that we make no mistake in viewing the shining promises of the documentalists as new lights on the horizon of librarianship, that we make our mistake in fearing that the documentalist will invade the domain of the generalist. I convince myself that he will not, and that we need both documentalist and generalist. I am not against communications. I am not against automation. I am not against documentalists. I am for books, for people, for ideas.

There is magic in something new. In the mid-twentieth

century television and electronic computers are new. But let us not forget that there may be magic also in something old. Have books lost their glamor because we have had them for five hundred years? There is a renewal of the magic of Gutenberg in every book that comes from the press. Television and electronic computers have a glamor only a few years old. If we had these things and did not have books, we would have to invent the book. And we would hail that invention as a marvellous achievement in the efficient packaging of knowledge. Imagine the sensation of learning of the use of movable type as a new discovery: how far-reaching it would seem. What avenues of imagination would open could we stand in the 1450's and think what the invention of printing would mean to world history! Is it an exaggeration to view it as comparable to the first fission of the atom, to pair Gutenberg and Fermi as architects of new worlds?

The glamor of the book does not end with its early history. There has been a constant advance in technical proficiency. There has been an evolution of bookmaking as an art. To the most seasoned author there is a thrill in seeing his words in print. The librarian can partake of this thrill, however vicariously, however slightly, each time he works with a book. A little of the glamor of literary creativity adheres to the librarian who knows that books are packages for ideas, are his bridges to people and to a new world of ideas beyond the dreams of all of us. Books must remain as individual as people, as individual as ideas. We can standardize our methods. Within restricted areas we can standardize our forms. Over a long period it may be possible for publishers to package the literature (if the base use of that word may be excused) into unitary parcels. Then automation will work. But let us not sell our birthright for a mess of package. Let us not try to standardize books, people, or ideas. Let us not try to make automatons of librarians.

We are not automatons. We should infuse into our professional life the same humanity we ourselves represent. Our library press is an example of our failure to do this. We take ourselves as librarians so very seriously in our research and writing that the charge that the Most Reverend John Wright, Bishop of Pittsburgh, made last year against education seems especially true of librarianship. "There is a deadly earnestness," he said, ". . . which suggests that knowledge and information may be on the increase and wisdom and understanding on the way out. . . . But one asks . . . why is it all so deadly earnest? What has become of the humanistic touch that used to betray a humane preoccupation and that revealed itself in an occasional trace of a sense of humor?" We write too much too soon. We write too much for ourselves—to the point sometimes of castigating the converted or of mumbling into our pillows. Are we so timorous of our status that we must spell out every commonsense routine in elaborate detail? Or are we so convinced of the sanctity of print that we believe publishing something makes it so? Whatever the causes, the result is a proliferation of redundant and repetitive articles. As an expression of the most literate profession our literature should be exceptionally thoughtful, exceptionally useful, and exceptionally literate. It is not.

What a poverty stricken, cliché-ridden mass of words library literature is! We have a literature of quantity, but have we a literature of quality? There is pressure to publish, but there is no equivalent pressure to write intelligently and well. In our profession there is not yet quite the pressure to publish for promotion that there is in more specialized academic disciplines. Do we not have a stronger charge as librarians than the members of any other profession to aim at a high level of literacy, at good writing which will also be good reading? Information is not enough. There are good periodicals and good books in library literature, but it is difficult to find them among the welter of the trivial, the repetitious; among the flow of printed speeches, how-we-do-it pieces, surveys and opinions stuffed and over-dressed with the impedimenta of scholarship.

This is the library press as we have made it in our rush to be "professional." There are exceptions, of course—the immensely improved *ALA Bulletin, Library Trends, The Library Quarterly,* but even in these cases one is reminded that

220 *Harwell*

in the land of the blind the one-eyed is king. We have the
talent and ability among our profession to have a fine, liter
ate body of writing. We fail librarianship if we do not exercise our talents and abilities to produce a library literature
worthy of the name.

FALSE HUMILITY
Our failure to achieve the literate, effective expression our
profession deserves is a symptom of a kind of false humility
that pervades our activities in many areas. We fail too often
to assert our abilities. Even more often we fail to seize the
opportunities for effectiveness through our own professional
organizations and through cooperative activities.

Librarians speak loud and clear of the great values of cooperation. Let them speak thus to the marines. Let them
speak to me again of cooperation when they have made it
work on the initiative of librarians. There are several fine
projects in library cooperation, but not one major cooperative project in library services has achieved even moderate
success without major financial support from outside sources,
and many of them have had their inception in the enthusiasm
and initiative of non-librarians. I think cooperation is wonderful. I think in cooperation lie many of the answers to library
problems. But cooperation is like democracy. It is much
easier to be democratic up the social scale than democratic
down. Until we get over our fear of being cooperated out of
something or, its corollary, of our hope of getting a free ride
by lip-service to cooperation, cooperation won't work. I
think librarians are big enough to make it work.

I think librarians are big enough to live up to the aims
and possibilities of our profession. I am not worried about
our academic status because I believe we can achieve—in some
cases have already—a more desirable status as librarians—if we
live up to our responsibilities and abilities.

Nor am I worried about our long-term potentialities as
recruiters. If we can emphasize the universals in librarianship
—the myriad aspects of its concern with books, people, and
ideas—we can attract the kind of recruits we need. We do not

want any others. Miss Elizabeth Nesbitt said at the Conference of Eastern College Librarians in 1955: "Librarians themselves have been guilty of emphasizing certain conditions and of resigned acceptance of these conditions, at the same time that they blame these conditions for lack of success in recruiting. . . . Librarians have been accused by their own colleagues and by non-librarians of being too apologetic about their profession, too much inclined to passive acceptance of remediable conditions, too little inclined toward militant assertion of the essential dignity and high importance of the library in such a society and such a world as exists today. It is possible that our lack of success in recruiting lies within ourselves."

I am not apologetic about librarians and librarianship, but I agree with the essence of Miss Nesbitt's statement. I think librarians are better than they know and that it is high time they learn how good they are and high time they let other people know how good they are.

How can we demonstrate how good we are? By being good librarians. But the answer really is not as simple as that. We must approach librarianship with a broad humanistic spirit. We must adapt to librarianship any and all devices and controls which further its purpose. We must emphasize quality in every area of our work, and especially in the writings which represent us to our colleagues in librarianship and to our colleagues in the whole field of education. We must work together, both in our professional organizations and in specific cooperative efforts. We must strive for status on our merits. And we must recruit on our merits.

We have our problems and I do not know the answers. But working together as librarians we can find the answers. It will be a privilege to participate in finding them. It is a privilege to be a part of the diurnal triangle of librarianship: people, ideas, and books.   □

ON THE GENTLE ART OF LIBRATING

Frances Farmer

The Twentieth Century is the great age of motion. Things were relatively quiet, or slow, shall we say, for the couple of centuries between Sir Isaac Newton and Albert Einstein, but as we passed Mid-Century the move was on. Gravity, in a sort of cold-war grip with velocity for a prolonged period of time, finally snapped and all sorts of barriers have been toppling ever since. Man in motion is the symbol of our time. Law Librarians must join the procession.

I do not know how we are to join the procession, but I suggest as a modest beginning that we need some kind of term which conveys the notion of motion—we need a verb. I have often wondered why we librarians do not have one. The teacher, we are told, "teaches," an administrator "administers," a skindiver "skindives," but alas, what do we do? How can we put ourselves on the move? How can we capture in one word the function of the librarian?

What we are looking for is a verb that is at once descriptive, appealing and a pace setter. I propose we put this problem on the agenda for a panel discussion at some future meeting. Meanwhile I offer, with exuberant humility, the product of my own brooding; a product compounded of earnest search, restless thought and sudden inspiration, to say nothing of that age old method called trial and error.

Reprinted from *Law Library Journal*, 52: 127-130, May 1959, by permission of the author and the publisher (American Association of Law Libraries).

First, I tried "librarianate" but discarded it as obviously lacking in elegance. I could not quite picture saying to the Dean of my Law School, "I'm sorry I cannot listen to you any longer as I must go librarianate." Somehow it seemed to miss the kind of authority our verb should command—the kind of word that would not exactly intimidate Deans, but which would produce a sense of restraint when they attempt to descend upon us with the bleak announcement that the book budget has just been cut.

Next I toyed with various versions of the Latin word *"liber"* and tried "liberate" (pronounced leeberate, if you like) but rejected it out of hand as being already preempted by victorious armies and Cuban revolutionaries.

Other possibilities of the "izing" and "iteing" variety presented themselves, but they smacked too much of plebeian connotations, bringing to the imagination cleaner sinks, white clothes and slicker floors. Hardly the type of word for the vaulted realms of the law library!

It is needless to go through the entire inventory of discarded candidates. Suffice it to say that late one evening following a frustrating session with a budget minded dean and an exasperating meeting with a hard-boiled dealer, the word came to me. I offer it *gratis* to Messrs. Funk and Wagnalls, Webster *et al.*, and also to my colleagues: the function of a librarian is "to librate."[1]

Consider for a moment the beauty of this terse verb. Not only is it descriptive, it also gathers added luster and momentum by a kind of symbiosis, that is, "to librate" suggests "to vibrate." Thus two thoughts are happily joined. We have our long missing verb and we are librarians on the move —truly a part of the great age of motion.

So much for our verb. What does it connote? In keeping with the famous dictum of Jackson who at the Battle of New Orleans exhorted his troops to "elevate them guns a little lower," let us consider our job at a modest level. Who are our tormentors and what problems do they pose? Roughly they fall into two broad groups or categories, the humanized and the de-humanized. Common to the former is the penetrating

observation made by my colleague, Paul Burton, at the
Chicago meeting in 1954 that

> . . . there is nothing wrong with law librarians that
> could not be cured by the extermination of
> judges, lawyers, legislators, general librarians, law
> professors and students, law book dealers and
> publishers, library committees and boards.[2]

This broadside, with which no discriminating law librarian will quibble deserves, however, to be made more explicit.
For the law school librarian I am inclined to think that the
genus homo that bears the closest scrutiny is the professor
not merely because he has faculty status but because of certain attributes which all appear to share. Whether they are
good professors, bad professors or medium professors, the
characteristic they share in common is the hoarding instinct.

In dealing with this special group, the art of librating
must meet its greatest challenge. To balance diplomacy with
sleight of hand is the only combination yet devised that will
serve to meet head on the compulsion of all professors to
keep as many library books as possible in their own offices
and in a manner designed to elude the public spirited librarian.

The hazard of the game is heightened, of course, when
the professor involved turns out to be a member, even the
chairman, of the Library Committee. More often than not it
is this alleged ally who is the worst offender. When you have
polished up your skill at retrieving countless books from his
shelves, without at the same time arousing his ill will, you
may allow yourself one fleeting moment's sense of gratifica-
tion that you are making some slight progress in the gentle
art of librating.

Reference to one other typical specimen among the professional group cannot be resisted. This is the quaint professor who once a year immediately prior to a peak load of
activity such as an examination period drops by your office
"to explore the possibilities of having all the books in my
course in one place instead of scattered throughout the
stacks, according to a scheme I've not yet seen any sense to!"
His grammar is obviously bad and you allow yourself a

moment's reflection upon your rating of his faculty status intellect.

Suddenly there flashes before your mental eye a portrait of this Mephistopheles out on the back parking lot crouched over a smouldering heap which upon closer inspection turns out to be the charred remains of your classification scheme! At that point your aroused temper generates sufficient electro-magnetic current to switch the picture: there *you* are on the *front* parking lot—Salome robed in veils and poised for a frenzied dance, but it is quite evident that the head on that platter does not belong to John the Baptist!

With the show over you patiently try to explain that the library is designed to serve normal people and not tax experts. With good luck, a winning smile and some double talk you may pacify this ingenious tormentor.

It must be willingly confessed, however, that not all of our tormentings originate with the faculty. That bold bustling breed, the younger offenders commonly known as students, are also past masters at the art.

The hoarding instinct of the faculty is matched, of course, by that of the students although here a different kind of game is involved. Not having offices for the most part, students resort to a kind of cat and mouse technique. This means that the harassed librarian is likely to find *Jones On Evidence* coyly placed next to Hobbes' *Leviathan* and *Williston On Sales* cheek by jowl with *Ram On Facts*.

So much for the so-called human side. The sun will never set on the day on which you will not be called upon to exercise your skill in the mechanical or applied arts, to describe these duties in the most respectable technical manner. Here all of your library training is just so much impedimenta.

In place of knowledge and skill in library techniques, the prime requirement is an elementary understanding of the field of engineering both mechanical and electrical which will prove rewarding when confronted with leaking plumbing and blown out electrical systems. A knowledge of chemistry will serve as a worthwhile weapon when sudden atmospheric conditions that not even an orbiting satellite could predict deposits blue mold on a substantial portion of the collection.

For such emergencies the librarian must possess the zeal of an adventurer enlightened and reinforced by a passion for scientific research and experimentation. Nor is this all. Vermin have a strong affinity for old English cases and some modern American treatises and, although you may not have had occasion to develop your technique to the degree of a commercial operator, you may discover that the skilled fumigator will require your services in catching, preserving and labelling specimens.

Meanwhile there are other phases of activity with built-in difficulties that demand attention. There is always the cash register. How can we accommodate all the frenzied pressures of faculty and book dealers on a budget pruned by non-book-ish legislators (where your institution depends upon the public purse), and how can we resist that special bargain—that something you don't need at a price you cannot resist? It could be so pleasant if only we were able to get the works to librate with abandon.

Alas, the librarian on the move must yet move cautiously and with discrimination and with a kind of informed intuition which directs that, while Book A may be good, Book B may be better. Here lies the necessary art—the art which defies a neat logarithmic solution. The exercise of this art requires knowledge of the total needs of the Law School as well as those of the library. That is why the librarian must always be an intimate partner in the life of the school—not merely a convenient administrative appendage. To librate in isolation is certainly not a valid concept for the mid-century librarian on the move—a fact which deans, faculties and other assorted adjuncts to a well run law library should by now begin to appreciate. □

[1] Our suggestion that the word be used to describe the function of a librarian may have been anticipated already. According to Webster, "to librate" means "to vibrate as a balance does before coming to rest; hence to be poised." Our suggested modification of this definition is simply to add after the word "poised" the explanatory dictum: "as in managing a law school library inhabited by faculties and students."

[2] 48 L. LIB. J. 364.

LAGNIAPPE

THE CRATE AT OUTPOST 1

Matthew Gant

The wind whistled through the valley, and the pyramidal tent that signified Outpost 1 quivered before the blast. As always, sentry Rudd placed his hand before the oil burner that feebly lit the interior of the tent, shielding the yellow flame from the stray gusts that whipped through the torn canvas. And, as always, he cast a quick, nearly guilty look at sentry Dennison, who lay fully dressed on a narrow cot in the rear of the tent.

"It won't fizz out," Dennison said. He lay on his back, his hands resting behind his head, and his eyes stared at the sloping ceiling. Occasionally he wiggled his fingers and watched with amusement the play of shadows on the canvas overhead.

"I know," Rudd said, biting his lip and looking away.

"Then why do you do it?" Dennison said.

"I don't know," Rudd said. He spread his hands.

Outside, the wind sank for a moment and from far off came the barking of dogs. Rudd shivered and drew the frayed collar of his parka close about him. He stole another quick look at Dennison, and then his eyes shifted to the corner of the tent just to the left of the doorway flap.

The crate was still there.

"What are you afraid of?" Dennison asked. "It won't move."

"I don't know," Rudd said, and then he flared for a moment. "It's our job. We must see the crate."

He stood up defiantly and strode to the crate. It squatted on the corner, four feet high, four feet long, four feet wide. It was of wood, nailed securely across the top.

Rudd remembered the last nailing detail. They had come in during the warm weather and ripped out the rusting nails with their hands. One of them had howled when a nail slipped and gashed his palm. The naildriver was the biggest man Rudd had ever seen. He pounded the new, shiny nails with the heel of his rifle, and soon the crate was nearly as good as new.

And while they had changed the nails, a two-striper had stood over the detail, with a rifle that shone dully in the flickering gloom of the tent.

Rudd had seen many nailing details come and go. The thought filled him with pride. Ever since they had landed on the island outpost, he and Dennison had been assigned to see the crate.

"You can see it from your bed," Dennison said, breaking the thoughts. "There's no rule about seeing it from your bed."

"I don't care," Rudd said. "It's easier to see from here."

Dennison said, "Ah-h-h," and the sound turned into a yawn. "Wake me when the two-striper comes," he said.

Rudd flinched. He wanted to tell Dennison that he was not to sleep on duty. Rudd was not supposed to see the crate alone. When the two-striper had told them the order, this had been emphasized:

"Never see the crate alone. Always make sure you're both seeing it at the same time. One man alone can't be trusted."

And both Dennison and Rudd had nodded, gravely.

But it was always the same. Dennison would sleep until the two-striper reached the flap and, cursing, tried to find the tent buttons. And Dennison would be on his feet, gripping his rifle, when the two-striper finally strode to the tent's center and reviewed his sentries.

Once Dennison hadn't been lucky. The two-striper had found the buttons quickly and the soft mud outside had cushioned his steps, and he was inside before Dennison woke. Dennison had to stand on his feet for a very long time after that.

And the two-striper had lectured him about the crate.

"Do you know why you're here, soldier?" the two-striper had asked Dennison.

"Yes," Dennison said. "To see the crate."

"And why see the crate?" the two-striper persisted.

"So nobody gets it," Dennison answered, his face reddening under the softly-spoken questions.

"And why should nobody get it?" the two-striper probed.

Dennison had stammered then and Rudd wanted to help him out, but he didn't want to have to stand for a very long time also. Besides, he did not know the answer.

"Because," the two-striper snapped. "That's why, you fool."

And Dennison repeated, "Because." And the two-striper imposed the sentence and left.

Later that night Rudd had whispered to Dennison, who stood there, his rifle clutched tight in his hands. "Are you awake?"

"Yes," Dennison had said.

"I was wondering," Rudd said. "I was wondering about something."

"You're always wondering about something," Dennison said. "What's it this time?"

"I was wondering because why," he said, his voice still a whisper in the pitch-black tent.

"Because why what?" Dennison asked harshly. "Because why what, you fool?"

"Nothing," Rudd said, and he turned to see the crate though it was too dark to make it out.

But gradually he found the nerve to ask, and Dennison,

who had been in the service far longer than he, and who was once a two-striper himself, finally told him.

"Because the crate was once owned by the enemy, long, long ago," he had said, and even Dennison, who slept when he should have been seeing the crate, let his eyes creep to the flap in case the two-striper, or, even worse, the yellow-bar were near.

"The enemy," Rudd had said, involuntarily, his eyes bugging.

"Shut up, you fool," Dennison hissed.

And many, many seasons of warm to cold had gone by before Rudd had asked more questions and learned more about why the crate had to be seen.

Dennison did not know the whole story, for no man did, he said.

But the facts were these: the crate contained an enemy weapon, an old and very powerful weapon, which must never be allowed to fall into his hands again. And during bad times, such as now when the dogs were out barking in pursuit of enemy smell, the crate had to be seen all the time so that nobody got it away.

It was as simple as that.

And from that time on, Rudd had felt the pride of his job, and he wondered even more strongly how Dennison could sleep when he ought to be seeing.

Especially during bad times, when the dogs were barking.

Rudd had never heard so much barking as these past nights. He wished, sometimes, he were back with the others, not at Outpost 1. Once, last warmth, he had become ill and a doctor had visited him, a one-striper. Before he had left, the doctor had told him of the others.

"They are sick-afraid," he had said. "They say the enemy is nearer."

But though for a moment Rudd, too, was sick-afraid, he laughed at the doctor. Doctors knew so little, especially about the movement of soldiers.

But when he told Dennison of it, Dennison didn't laugh. He sat and stared through the open flap at the sun skinking behind the peaks.

And now, the dogs were barking as never before. And the two-striper had come in twice this night, instead of once, and even though their share of oil had been burned up, he had brought more. "See the crate," he said, shortly, as he left.

And Rudd saw the crate, and even Dennison lay there on his bed, his eyes wide open.

They were not relieved until the sun was high the next day.

And that night when they returned to the tent, the two-striper handed them each a bullet for their rifles. It was the first time either man had ever held a loaded rifle.

"See the crate," the two-striper had said fiercely before he left, "see the crate." And Rudd noticed the dark circles under the two-striper's eyes.

"These are bad times," Rudd said to Dennison, staring at him anxiously.

"Bad," Dennison repeated.

"Do you think—?" Rudd started.

"Do I think what, you fool?" Dennison said. But his voice was not sharp at all.

"Do you think the enemy is coming?"

Outside the wind howled again, howled loud, but even over the howl came the sound of the dogs.

"I don't know," Dennison had said, at last.

Rudd quickly put his hand over the oil burner to shield it from the wind, but this time Dennison didn't say anthing. Things were bad, Rudd knew.

He stood straight and he thought: I will do my job. He walked to the crate and leaned on it.

"Don't touch it, you fool," Dennison said.

"But why?" Rudd asked, puzzled. He had touched it many times before, feeling the creaking wood and sometimes he had peeled splinters of wood from the crate and used them to make pictures in the mud outside.

"Ah-h-h," Dennison said. "Just don't."

And Rudd walked away, ashamed.

Suddenly the outside quivered with noise. The dogs were nearby now, and there must have been dozens of them, yapping and howling, and Dennison said, "Listen."

"The barking is loud," Rudd said.

"No, not the barking. I can hear them gnashing their teeth."

Rudd listened and he heard, too, and he thrilled to the sound. "The enemy will never get to us, not with those dogs of ours," he boasted.

And through the sound came the clomping of a man's heavy boots, running in thick mud.

"The enemy!" Rudd said, his hands tightening over the stock of the rifle, his hand reaching for the bolt.

But it wasn't the enemy. It was a one-striper, the runner from the others.

He stood swaying in the center of the tent, a huge man with a black beard, his eyes red-rimmed and circled with the same sort of black lines, though even deeper, as those about the two-striper's.

"Is this it?" he panted, pointing to the crate. It had been many seasons since Rudd had seen the runner, and he looked much older, and Rudd felt sorry that the runner didn't even remember the crate.

"Yes," he said. "That's it."

The runner stood there and the tent was still. He bent once and lightly moved his hand toward the crate, and then drew it back quickly. He spun on his heavy boots and faced the sentries.

"You must run," he said. "We are beaten."

"Beaten?" Rudd said. "I don't believe it."

Dennison stared at the runner and then he sat on his cot and started to pull on his boots. "Come on," he said to Rudd, "we don't have all night."

"But—"

"Beaten," the runner insisted.

"And the crate?" Rudd said. "The crate?"

"Destroy it," the runner said. "Quickly. You have no time. You must go to the hills when you have finished. Do you have enough oil?"

Rudd stared at the lamp which flared full and strong.

"No, you fool," Dennison said, "not for the lamp. For the crate. The enemy must not get the crate."

The runner handed Rudd a can of oil, and with his bayonet, ripped it open. He stood at the flap for a long moment, and then he raised his hand to his eyes. "Good-by," he said, "and hurry."

Rudd stared at the open can of oil, and then he started to pour it on the wooden slats across the top of the crate. The barking was frantic now, yards away it seemed.

Dennison tore the can from his hand. "No," he panted, "there must be something inside the wood that can't be destroyed this way, wet packing or metal or something. We'll have to remove the top." He reached for the wood and started to pull at the slats.

"No," Rudd said. "We're not allowed to. We must see the crate, not the inside."

But Dennison would not be stopped, and Rudd watched as the slats groaned and pulled up sharply. Some cracked in Dennison's hands as he clawed at them, and suddenly, the last two slats came up together and the top was off.

They moved back a pace and looked down. There was a sheet of yellowed paper, with five black marks on it, over the inside of the crate, and Dennison reached out and grabbed it away and they both leaned forward to see.

They looked up at each other, and there was a frown on each forehead. Inside the crate were box-like things, most of them the length of a man's hand span, maybe a little longer, not quite as wide, and two, three fingers deep. Each one was covered with cloth.

There were steps outside now, and the dogs were no longer near, their barking off down the valley.

Dennison screamed once, in rage and fear, and he sprinkled oil frantically on the top of the box-like things and he sprinkled oil on the yellowed paper with the five black marks, and he thrust the paper into the oil lamp until a corner caught fire.

Then he threw the burning paper on top of the crate, and they both raced from the tent for the hills.

And as Rudd ran, he was sick-afraid, and even many seasons later while he hid in the woods, he still remembered with cringing fear the crate, and sometimes when he found himself drawing in the mud, the thing he drew was the five black marks that had been on the yellowed paper covering the things inside—

BOOKS   ☐

THE CONTRIBUTORS

Lester Asheim — Professor, Graduate Library School, University of Chicago — received the 1973 Beta Phi Mu Award for distinguished service to education for librarianship. He is author of *Librarianship in the Developing Countries* (1966).

Margaret Bennett is the pseudonym of June Biermann and Barbara Toohey, members of the library staff at Los Angeles Valley College, Van Nuys, California. They have contributed articles and essays to a number of magazines including *Atlantic Monthly*, *Library Journal*, *Redbook*, *Saturday Review*, and *Writer's Digest*.

June Biermann, with Barbara Toohey, writes under the pseudonym Margaret Bennett.

Catherine Drinker Bowen — known first for a volume of autobiographical essays titled *Friends and Fiddlers* (1935) — received the National Book Award for Non-Fiction in 1958 for *The Lion and the Throne: The Life and Times of Sir Edward Coke* (1957). She is also author of *Yankee from Olympus* (1944), *John Adams and the American Revolution* (1950), *Miracle at Philadelphia* (1966), *Biography: The Craft and the Calling* (1969), *Family Portrait* (1970).

Ray L. Carpenter is Associate Professor, School of Library Science, University of North Carolina, Chapel Hill, North Carolina. With James Lewis, he has translated and edited José Ortega y Gasset's "The Mission of the Librarian."

Verner W. Clapp, full-time consultant to the Council on Library Resources and its president from 1956 to 1967, died on June 15, 1972. For some thirty-five years (1922-56) he was a member of the staff of the Library of Congress. He is author of *The Future of the Research Library* (1964) and *Copyright: A Librarian's View* (1968). He received the 1960 Joseph W. Lippincott Award for distinguished service to the library profession.

Hardin Craig, Jr., Librarian of the Fondren Library, Rice University, Houston, Texas, from 1953 to 1968 died on June 28, 1971. Dr.

Craig's previous position at Rice was that of Associate Professor of History from 1946 to 1953.

Frances Farmer is Professor of Law and Law Librarian, University of Virginia, Charlottesville, Virginia.

Ilo Fisher is Special Projects Librarian at Wittenberg University in Springfield, Ohio.

Matthew Gant is the pen name of a free-lance writer who lives in southern California. Under this pseudonym he has published *The Raven and the Sword* (1960), a novel based on the life of Sam Houston.

Charlotte Georgi is Chief Librarian of the Graduate School of Business Administration at the University of California at Los Angeles. She previously held administrative positions in the University of North Carolina Library and taught at Stephens College, Columbia, Missouri.

Richard Barksdale Harwell — formerly Associate Executive Director of the American Library Association and Executive Secretary of the Association of College and Research Libraries — is Librarian, Georgia Southern College, Statesboro, Georgia. An authority on the Civil War and Reconstruction periods in American history, he is author or compiler of *The Confederate Reader* (1957), *The Union Reader* (1958), *The War They Fought* (1960), *The Confederate Hundred* (1964).

R. J. Heathorn could not be identified in any of the several biographical sources of information consulted. The Librarian of *Punch*, where "Learn with BOOK," originally appeared, was unable to supply any biographical information. If any reader has information (however brief) about RJH, the editor of this volume would be delighted to receive it and to know the source of the biographical data.

Quincy Howe — news analyst for CBS (1942-49) and ABC (1954-63) — is the author of seven books including *Blood Is Cheaper Than Water* (1939) and *Ashes of Victory: World War II and Its Aftermath* (1972). He has received the George Foster Peabody Award (1955) and the Overseas Press Club Award (1959) for radio-tv news analysis, and in 1962 he won the Columbia-Catherwood Award for responsible international journalism.

James Lewis is a member of the Law Library staff, University of North Carolina, Chapel Hill, North Carolina. With Ray L. Carpenter, he has translated and edited José Ortega y Gasset's "The Mission of the Librarian."

G. D. Lillibridge is Professor of American History at Chico State College, Chico, California.

José Ortega y Gasset (1883-1955) — Spanish essayist and philosopher — is known chiefly for *The Revolt of the Masses* (1932). He is also author of *Man and People* (1957) and *Man and Crisis* (1958).

Lawrençe Clark Powell is Dean Emeritus of the School of Library Service, University of California at Los Angeles. In 1960 he received from the American Library Association the first Clarence Day Award for the encouragement of a love of books and reading. Among his more recent books are *Bookman's Progress* (1968), *Fortune and Friendship* (1968), *The Example of Miss Edith M. Coulter* (1969), *California Classics* (1971), *The Desert As Dwelled On* (1973).

William Ready is Professor of Bibliography and Librarian at McMaster University, Hamilton, Ontario, Canada. He is author of *The Reward of Reading* (1964), *The Tolkien Relation* (1968), *Necessary Russell* (1969). He received the American Library Association's Clarence Day Award in 1961.

Peter J. Rosenwald, formerly Business Manager of the Book Division, American Heritage Publishing Company, Inc., is a consultant on general international publishing operations and direct mail order marketing. He represents Wunderman, Ricotta and Kline (New York City) in Europe, and makes his home in London. He is International Arts Critic for *The Wall Street Journal*.

Jennifer Savary (formerly M. J. Savary) is the author of *The Latin American Cooperative Acquisitions Program: An Imaginative Venture* (1968) and now lives in Norfolk, England. For a number of years she worked for the United Nations in New York City.

Louis Shores is Dean Emeritus, School of Library Science, Florida State University, Tallahassee, Florida. Among his books are *Basic Reference Sources* (1954), *Mark Hopkins' Log and Other Essays* (1965), *Library-College USA* (1970), *Library Education* (1972). He received in 1967 the Isadore Gilbert Mudge Award for distinguished contributions to reference librarianship and also the Beta Phi Mu Award for distinguished service to education for librarianship. His *Looking Forward to 1999*, a novel, was published in 1972.

Barbara Home Stewart is a library public relations executive for J. B. Lippincott Company, Philadelphia, Pennsylvania.

Barbara Toohey, with June Biermann, writes under the pseudonym Margaret Bennett.

Edwin Wolf 2nd is Librarian of The Library Company of Philadelphia. He is author (with John F. Fleming) of *Rosenbach: A Biography* (1960).

A NOTE ABOUT THE EDITOR

John David Marshall is University Librarian, Middle Tennessee State University, Murfreesboro, Tennessee. He is a graduate of Bethel College (McKenzie, Tennessee) and of the School of Library Science, Florida State University (Tallahassee, Florida). A contributor of articles and book reviews to a number of professional and literary journals, he has also written or edited ten books including *Books-Libraries-Librarians* (1955), *Of, By, and For Librarians* (1960), *An American Library History Reader* (1961), *Louis Shores: A Bibliography* (1964), *Mark Hopkins' Log and Other Essays by Louis Shores* (1965), *A Fable of Tomorrow's Library* (1965), *Approaches to Library History* (1966). He has served two terms as Secretary of the American Library History Round Table, and since 1966 he has been Book Review Editor for the *Journal of Library History*. He is Chairman of the University and College Library Section of the Southeastern Library Association for 1972-74.

AUTHOR - TITLE INDEX

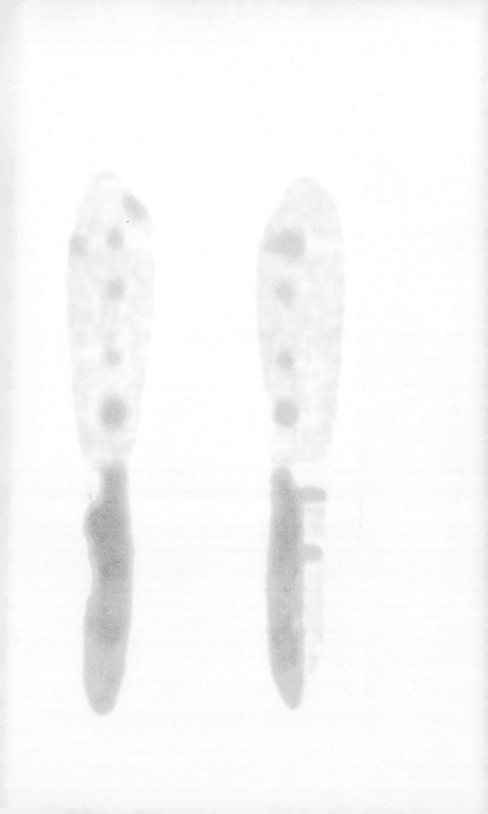

DATE DUE
